Tales of a

Reluctant

Psychic

By Mari Schoenzeit

Tales of a Reluctant Psychic

By Mari Schoenzeit

Wolfdancer Publishing
P.O. Box 4581
Durango, Colorado 81302
1st Edition
ISBN-10: 0-9968760-2-2
ISBN-13: 978-0-9968760-2-5

Acknowledgements

Thank you, Wolfdancer Publishing, for the encouragement, direction, and editorial support you consistently provided, helping this book come to life and become the tale that it was meant to be.

Author's Note

The stars are surrounded by darkness. Look to the light, seek the light, follow the light, and be wary of anything else. Use discernment and good judgment as you develop your own intuitive abilities. No course of action should be taken unless it is kind, positive, peaceful, helpful, and gentle. Evaluate your thoughts, your insight, and your words and actions in terms of how they serve the highest good.

When in doubt, pray and ask to be filled with love, joy, truth, peace, and compassion. I believe that prayers are answered, but we must learn to listen carefully, to quiet our inner rant, and to consciously choose to think about and focus on the best that we find in the present moment.

May all of your choices be grounded in integrity. May the path you choose to follow be one of service, a path that honors forgiveness and the goodness and wisdom in yourself and in the world.

With peace and well-wishes,
Mari

Dedication

This book is dedicated to my mother, so recently crossed into the light. Thank you for waiting until I was able to get there to be at your side to hold your hand as you embarked upon the next phase of your journey. Thank you, too, for all of the years that came before that.

This book is also dedicated to my aunt, my second mother, who seemed to be in a hurry to join her sister. Thank you for giving me, your children, and your friends a chance to say a final good-bye despite your readiness to head into the Light.

These sisters seemed unable to have a superficial conversation, taking ideas deeper, seeking to understand other people, and teaching their children, those birthed and those nurtured and guided, to ask good questions, to find ways to give to the world, and to learn compassion. I am grateful to have been a daughter to you both. Peace and love on the path ahead.

Preface

I have tried my best to protect everyone, their identities and their privacy, mentioned in these "tales." I have changed every name, I have obscured dates and locations, but I have not altered the salient facts. All events are described as accurately as possible given the fickleness of memory and the passage of time. Similarly, dialogues are recreations based on memory. Once in a while the words recorded here are a verbatim recounting of what was said or heard, the actual words having been etched into my mind with such clarity that their complete retrieval was easy. At other times the words and dialogue presented are simply as close to what was said as I can recall. I strive for candor throughout this book and leave it to readers to understand this story in ways that make sense, or perhaps make no sense to them at all, engaging imagination more than reason, the heart more than the head.

I was a hardened skeptic until it became simply too illogical and unreasonable, silly, even, to maintain that stance. However, I believe that that skepticism, overall, has served me well, has helped me to be a more analytical reader and thinker and to develop an expanded and evolving world view, bit my bit, by asking questions, by challenging accepted opinion and dogma alike, by questioning my own beliefs, and by learning to think and act for myself. It is central to my personal philosophy to embrace a worldview that is still forming. I have a point of view, at least at a given moment, but I do not ultimately know what I believe. Belief is something that I want to hold softly and with a light and laughing heart.

Genuine knowing and understanding of the nature of God, of what constitutes Truth, of what is ultimately real, stretches past the reach of my limited human mind. However, the seeking of deeper knowing, of a broader connection to wisdom, is an adventure that will continue, I hope, for the rest of my life and into the uncharted waters beyond.

Ultimately I think that the highest path one can choose involves releasing, little by little, as one is ready, all that we think we know about the world, about what can and cannot be, about truth, and about all that we think we understand concerning ourselves and why we're here. We let go and open as we embrace the unknown and unknowable.

This deeper quest reminds me of the traditional Buddhist image of an empty rice bowl. Rather than thinking we're really smart, rather than believing that we already know what's true, what's false, what's real, and what's impossible, sitting with a bowl (or mind or belief system) full of facts and opinions, instead we sit, with as much humility as we can muster, before the divine, our "bowl" or thoughts and emotions or point of view resting empty in our upturned hands. We open ourselves to listen so that we can be filled up, gradually, not with more of ourselves or our ancestors or accumulated statistics, dates, and lists of information, but with the stuff of the divine; here we're not seeking the little truths, but Light, Love, Wisdom, and Truth itself.

I love books and I've learned much from them, but experience is the greater teacher. I've been stubborn as I've gone through life, unwilling to accept an idea or alter a belief until I'd directly had a contradictory and more expansive experience myself. Sometimes, even then, while staring at impossible events I myself had witnessed and lived, I refused to shift, to change my mind or broaden my worldview.

Spirit, fortunately, has been patient with me, supportive, and endlessly forgiving as I've banged my head against personal experience, against who I thought I was and what I thought I knew. The divine realm always gave me another opportunity to learn the same lesson, then another and another chance until, finally, I absorbed that particular teaching and was ready to move on to yet another lesson, to face another obstacle, to stare down another fear until it gave up its gifts under pressure like carbon forming diamond. This never-ending curriculum was designed by a wise and patient Teacher. I am grateful for all I've learned and all that I've been able to let go of. Mostly, I'm excited about all that I'm yet to discover.

Perhaps, as you read these pages, you will remember some of the instances when you were speaking with angels, were guided by star-stuff. Your sense of the miraculous might expand. Your sense of the possible might blossom at the same time as old, limiting beliefs drop away to be replaced by a new and more radiant sense of yourself and this lifetime. It is my hope that as you read this book your experience of the unknown will grow and your connection to the limitless expanses and depths of creativity within you will open, revealing a more peaceful and joyful sense of all that you are and who you are meant to be.

"When in doubt, pray. When certain, pray harder."

Mari

Table of Contents

Home Port

I was raised with the idea that we are each meant to carve out a path for ourselves in life, finding a career, a home, a mate, a purpose and sense of direction that we select based on our interests, on our abilities, and on choices that appeal to us. According to this model, our choices are shaped by our family circumstances and values along with the opportunities that present themselves–maybe even by some luck. However, our lives and life path, from the big decisions like partners and work, to the little daily choice points, like what to say or not say to the people in line at the grocery store–those are all up to us. In this worldview we decide what our lives mean and what they're going to be about. We are the masters of our own destiny, the shapers of lives of free will and independent choice, the captains of our fate. In this view we are each at the helm of our own ship, setting goals and destinations for ourselves, choosing our ports of call, whom to let on board and whom to make walk the plank as we make our way into new waters and explore the world in which we find ourselves.

Sailors have traditionally charted their course by the stars. By eye alone or through the use of instruments such as the sextant, they followed Venus, the Morning Star, watched for the Big and Little Dippers, and were on friendly terms with star clusters and the planets, using these stellar arrangements to steer their ship. They knew that they also needed to pay close attention to the weather, to the signs augured by the sky and water around them, to watch the flight of birds, the movements of waves, and the creatures of the sea. They knew that while they might have goals and a destination in mind, their actual choices and the course taken would depend, perhaps entirely, on forces of nature and their reading of patterns of bird flight and the turning of the waves. These seafarers understood that elements beyond themselves had more power than they did and that they needed to watch and learn from these larger powers and portents in the world, from these signs offered to the observant. While intrepid, the mariners were humbled by the enormity of the sea. In the presence of its power, in the face of forces, seen and unseen, that shaped and determined the paths of their lives, they sailed with the current. They propelled their ships forward in favorable winds and sheltered in quiet coves during stormy times.

Sailors learned from the knowledge of those who came before, and unlike a modern teenager who might be quite sure to be in possession of all the answers and who is certain of his or her superiority over parental figures, sailors were dependent for their very lives on the maps of land forms and charts of shoals and perilous waters created by their predecessors. Maps, perhaps like parents, like one's elders, like the accumulated knowledge and experience of one's culture and ancestral group, although understood to often contain inaccuracies, were treasured possessions and studied carefully. Mariners traded stories, searched lore and myth for clues to dangers and hidden treasures, and felt themselves one with the elements that surrounded them and which determined their fortunes.

After many years of trying to chart my own course, with results that ranged from the ordinary to the disastrous, I finally learned that if I'm to successfully navigate this earthly lifetime, I need the help of the majestic powers that surround me, that surround us all, and that, if we pay attention, are giving us signals, are trying to teach us, are there to help us map our way in life. We are all mystical sailors learning to find personal balance in the midst of a shifting sea while observing the wind, the light, the quality of the air, and the color and feel of the waters around us. Rather than trying to live lives isolated from nature and disconnected from the powers that surround us, we can learn to watch the changing seasons and the birds and other creatures with which we share this watery terrain. We can begin to listen, to discern, to sense, to see, feel, and intuit, more and more deeply, the signs around us. As we become wiser we learn to follow the stars.

Hoist the Sails

I went to Gabrielle's wedding when I was 21. It was a beautiful summer day, and I was at my parent's home for a visit. Gabrielle was three years older and had grown up not far from where we lived. In addition to being a neighbor, I thought of her as a friend. I didn't think of her as a friend because we were close or had spent a lot of time together. We weren't and we hadn't. I thought of her as a friend almost involuntarily. I thought of her as a friend the way I imagine almost everyone who knew her did, because of her friendly and welcoming personality. Of course she was my friend! She made me feel as if the fact that we barely knew one another was simply an oversight, that time had gotten away from us, that circumstances had dictated limited contact, but naturally, we were friends. An informal survey of everyone she'd ever met would probably show that legions of other neighbors, acquaintances, coworkers, classmates, and co-parishioners felt the same way. We have all known people like this, those whose influence on our lives is disproportionate to how long or well we know them. Their impact continues to lap at the shores of our life and thought long after they've crossed the river.

After the church ceremony we returned to Gabrielle's family home for the reception. I was wearing a blue and white striped dress with puffy shoulders, which, I shudder to remember, was actually in style in the early 80's. The party blended elegance with informality, and everyone was having a good time, mingling and periodically visiting the tables set with food.

When the time came to toss the bouquet, the single women gathered below the outdoor balcony from which it would be thrown, jockeying for advantage, eagerly awaiting their chance to grab the symbol of imminent marriage. In fact, the competition looked quite intense, with fit, athletic women in their wedding finery, hose, and heels, maneuvering for position. They were laughing, enjoying the game and the fun. I did see a couple of ladies whose eyes gleamed with fierce anticipation, though; they wanted to marry, they wanted the bouquet, and it might be advisable for others to steer clear.

I wanted the bouquet too, but in the more general sense of wanting to marry some day. Marriage and children still felt a long way off, remote. I decided not to join all of the others in the bouquet catch. I was shy and self-conscious, and anyway I thought that it wasn't really right for me to try to catch the bouquet since I didn't see myself marrying any time soon. I moved away from the balcony, off to the side of the house, to stand by the hors d'oeuvres and the men–not such a bad place from which to watch the festivities.

Mermaids and Sirens

The first throw from this bride who had clearly never mastered the back-handed toss, fell straight down to the ground, far from all of the waiting women. The bouquet was handed to a little girl of three or four to take back upstairs for a rematch. The child quickly got into the spirit of the game and sprinted inside and up the stairs to the new bride. A few moments later Gabrielle emerged on the balcony again, laughing, but with a determined look on her face. The guests resumed their places, including the little girl, who now stood ready under the balcony. This was a fun game, and it wasn't often that you got to play catch with a whole bunch of grown-ups. She probably wanted to catch that bouquet as much as any of the ladies-in-waiting.

The bride, who surpassed me in athletic ability, but perhaps not by much, put a lot of effort into her next throw. This time the flowers were going to hit their mark! The bouquet shot out of her hand off hard to the right and went rushing along the side of the house, far from the entire pack of single women. They followed the bouquet's flight, arms raised, looking up, heads turning as they watched it soaring high above them. I can't prove that the bouquet defied the laws of physics, but its path seemed to curve, and, in retrospect, its trajectory seemed anything but random. The bouquet came racing straight at my head. I caught it abruptly, just in time to keep it from impaling me between the eyes. I had no choice–it was catch the bouquet or be pierced by it. Since it's a long-standing belief of mine that it's bad form to be rushed off, bloody, to the hospital in the middle of a wedding reception, I caught the bouquet; I grabbed the thing in self-defense.

The ensuing events seemed simultaneously to occur both instantly and in slow motion. A crowd had gathered around me. People wanted to know whether I had even wanted the bouquet, why I hadn't stood with all of the other women if I did, and was I going to keep it? There were a few mingled congratulations. Some of the mothers of the women who had been waiting properly to catch the bouquet, right where they were supposed to, seemed particularly outraged. The comment of whether or not I might be a lesbian was pitched at me with all of the rest in rapid-fire succession. I answered yes and no and I don't know and I was busy trying to explain that I had meant yes to her question, but no to the other one. The little girl ran up to me. I leaned toward her to show her the bouquet and in my sweetest talking-to-a-little-girl voice I said, "Isn't it pretty?" Pretty was not the issue. She'd figured out that this game was played with an intense fervor. She snatched the bouquet from my hands and, dodging a sea of legs, ran into the house and up the stairs. I tried to get the flowers back from her, but she was playing this relay for keeps, far too fast and small for me to reach in time. Someone said that I must not have wanted the bouquet. I protested that I did want it, but it was too late. The crowd disbanded and regrouped around the young women who, having recognized me as being off-sides, had reformed into a tight squad beneath the balcony. A moment later the bouquet was thrown again, this time in a perfect, gentle arc, to one of the women below. I watched this scene as if from a great distance, still startled by the sudden winning and losing of the promise of marriage.

As I watched the bouquet land in another woman's hands, I heard a voice speak to me. It wasn't my voice and it wasn't spoken by anyone around me. It was a voice spoken somewhere in the air, a little off to my right. The tone was gentle, yet firm and authoritative. It said very clearly, calmly, and with complete surety, "The first one will be taken from you."

Red Sky In Morning,

Sailors Take Warning

The voice wasn't mean, although its message seemed cruel to me–and utterly clear. I knew exactly what it meant. I would get married and then my husband would die. The first one would be taken from me. The voice didn't offer a choice about it or suggestions on how to avoid this sad fate; it merely apprised me of the facts. More subtle than the voice informing me of the early departure of my first husband was the gentler knowing that accompanied it, letting me know that there would be a second husband as well, a "keeper."

Apparently this wasn't going to be a buffet line where I could pick and choose from a wide selection. This was some sort of school cafeteria from hell, and the lunch lady had just handed me my tray with the mystery meat special piled up high on it. "Eat up, dear," I could imagine this hair-netted vision with thick hands stuffed into little plastic sanitary gloves saying to me as she thrust it over the counter with a grimace. I had wanted white linen tablecloths and candles with small vases of flowers on the table. A discreet waiter, having been sent over especially by the maître d', would lean toward me and gently ask if I'd decided what I would like. Isn't that how life worked? We determined whom to marry, the type of career to pursue, where to live, whether or not to have children. Sure, accidents happened beyond our control, but basically, life was our oyster and we were king of the sea.

Somehow, age 21 seemed rather young to have one's belief in self-sovereignty snatched away so abruptly. No, this was not self-serve. This was a pre-packed lunch, made by my Father with love, but of which I was expected to eat every bite. I pictured the lunch lady watching me as I walked my tray over to an empty seat. Looking back over my shoulder at this divine messenger, her face seemed softer, her eyes (did I really give her gray cat-eye glasses?) more compassionate, but I didn't think she'd let me furtively toss a single item from my neon plastic tray into a nearby bin. I was on a special diet for life, it would seem. I supposed, being heaven-sent, that it would be well-balanced, and perhaps even ultimately nutritious, but that didn't mean that I wasn't reluctant to go about eating this meal which I knew contained a little bit too much organic matter for my taste. I had the feeling that some of it might be hard to digest as well.

Tacking Into The Wind

I've heard people speak about the day their lives changed forever. Usually such a comment follows a major event: the death of a loved one, the meeting of that special person, the moment when they were discovered by Hollywood while drinking a strawberry malt cream at the counter of the local hop shop. Those are all big things. Epic moments delivered in the usual carefully-wrapped packages. We're not the same after experiences of that nature.

I wonder, though, how often much more subtle turns in the wheel of fate move the mountain of our lives. The brush of a butterfly wing, a moment spent gazing at silent water pooling by our shoe, a quick little wink from God, and the wheel moves imperceptibly one hundredth of a millimeter to the right, sending us reeling off on a new vector, forever changed, soaring through the night sky.

I think back to the time before the day I caught the fickle bouquet. I was an atheist then. I should capitalize that. I was an Atheist then. That's better. I practiced an adamant, self-righteous Atheism, as certain in my beliefs as any hard-core fundamentalist.

It all seems pretty funny to me now. How quaint. I didn't know. I didn't have a clue in that analytical, prep-school prepped, elite college-entwined brain, so certain of its certainty. I was sure that the answer to every question, the meaning in every nuanced moment, could be found, dissected, and proven by the power and might of almighty science.

Don't get me wrong–I love science. All of it, that is, except maybe entomology. Bugs are icky. But science, that great cross-pollinating hive of analysis and deduction, I find utterly fascinating, and I periodically rue the twist of fate that sent me away from its study. I am still a closet geologist, ignorant of its deeper secrets, but endlessly fascinated by rock formations, silica, and butte. Don't even get me started on volcanoes.

I find biology riveting and chemistry alchemical. Physics surely holds the coded key to the physical universe. Love it. But… A small word, just three letters long, but *but* is a really big *but*. This butt with a wedgie trudged into a refined wedding party wearing too-tight jeans that were poorly hemmed. High-waters preparing for a flood. I was in deep.

What do you do when your comfy old belief system has been smashed to the proverbial smithereens in a single instant? Certainty? Gone. The supremacy of logic and reason? Uh-uh. How does one gracefully let go of the very essence of one's worldview without having a nervous breakdown or, at the very least, vomiting while breaking out into hives? It's hard to realize that one has been deeply wrong. Completely and utterly and totally, fundamentally, butt wrong. *Fundament* means "bottom," by the way, and in terms of my belief system, that's what I'd hit.

I carried shards of my old beliefs around for years, unable to let them go completely and also unable to embrace a radically new thought system, one that involved unseen factors I couldn't control. There were more participants in my life than just me? Others had an opinion? Who were these interested parties? Did I have a producer? A director?

Who had a front row seat in the arena of my small dramas? There was definitely someone else there, and this someone was eating my popcorn and talking during the movie. It was all highly irregular and unnerving.

In short, I was faced with the shocking realization that there was something bigger and more powerful than my brain. Or Einstein's brain. Or anyone's brain, logic, plans, or reason. No matter how long and hard we thought about it, the ultimate *it*, we weren't going to be able to figure *it* out. There was an unfathomable mystery at the center of our existence, and it was powerful, literally, beyond belief. For better or for worse, this something had taken a direct interest in my life.

Castaway

Of course, it seemed too incredible to think that the entire bouquet toss had been orchestrated just to give me this message of death. Who else received messages, however subtle, that day? Information flows through all of us in the form of radio waves, televised reruns, light, subatomic particles–a continuous stream of informational bibs and bobs courses through and around us. A web of relationships, information, and visible and invisible connections links us all. Suddenly I didn't see separate people at the reception, but patterns of people and events weaving through one another. Okay, a tapestry.

I wondered whether there had also been a message for the woman who caught the bouquet on the third throw, standing just where she should. Would there be a couple of close calls prior to marriage, nearly getting married twice before finally meeting her ultimate mate? Was she being taught patience, athleticism, and perseverance?

Was there a message for Gabrielle, the bride who unknowingly participated in sending me a message of a first marriage accompanied by a sad ending? Gabrielle's marriage would end too soon as well, in her case by her own early exit from this lifetime. Cancer would claim her long before her children, family, and friends were ready to say good-bye.

Were Gabrielle and I connected in this interlacing of life and wedding, celebration and premature departure?

What about the little girl who served as messenger? She was a tiny, persistent, feisty sprite, acting as my personal Hermes in miniature. Were there messages in all sorts of events and in the seemingly innocuous utterances of strangers and friends alike? Was I reading too much into this?

The voice at the wedding told me of a future event, of the death of someone I didn't even know, and since I had neither boyfriend nor crush, I couldn't imagine who this eventual husband might be. Someone I hadn't met yet, I supposed. But then, it wouldn't be fair to marry him, would it? I mean, it seemed like a death sentence. Whoever married me was going to die. Well, that was utterly ridiculous. I didn't have that kind of power over the lives of others and I definitely didn't want it. Did that mean that no matter what I did in my life, no matter where I lived or where I went, there would be only one person I could possibly marry? Or were there two or three possibilities, all of them currently incubating dreaded diseases? Should I start taking transatlantic flights during bird flu season in order to meet that perfect someone?

Maybe there would only be one person whom I would wish to marry? Maybe this person was already sick or maybe his heredity destined him to an early death? Actually, why should I assume that the first husband would die young? Perhaps he would live into his seventies and then I would marry again briefly before I died myself? However, just as I knew, in the core of my being, that this day's message was meant for me, and that it held the horrible guarantee that my first husband would die, it was also equally clear to me that he would die young. How harsh, to me and particularly to whomever I was going to marry.

There had to be a way to avoid this fate. I decided

that I would have to be careful about whom I married. He would have to be extremely healthy and come from a steady line of long-lived people. Some people marry for riches or for wit; I would marry for longevity. Yet, there were still freak accidents, electrocutions, murders, car wrecks, shark attacks, natural disasters. The list of possible ways to die suddenly seemed endless and equally uncontrollable. How could you decide how long you or someone else would live or how you would each meet your end? These decisions were clearly not under individual control, but was there someone who was in charge who held the cards of fate and who knew the progressions and eventual outcome of every one of our lives? I also began to wonder whether if we really knew exactly what was waiting in store for us through the course of our lives, would we still have the courage to live them?

I would return to these sorts of questions over and over again. If I'm not in charge, who is? And whose voice was it that spoke to me? Was it God? That seemed unlikely. Was Elijah, the prophet visitor of the Passover Seder, coasting along by my side generally, but not always, silent? Was a deceased relative giving me a heads up? "Just thought you'd like to know…"

The voice didn't belong to anyone I knew, alive or otherwise. The voice wasn't Godlike (Yes, you're wondering, what, exactly, does "Godlike" sound like? Can't really answer that–it's just sort of a vibe you get), but it wasn't fully human either. It was somewhere in between. Before this day I hadn't even believed in God (although I spoke to him from time to time, furtively, during the occasional adolescent emergency), and now I was considering the possible existence of a whole range of beings, disincarnate, and with the ability to communicate. It was turning into quite a day.

Finally I decided that it must have been an angel who spoke to me. "Angel" was a word that I knew, and since I did not, nor do I now, have a better explanation, "angel" seems to be the best, or at least the most "logical" (can one be logical when speaking of angels?) explanation. In any case, that's the word I'm going to use. That, and lunch counter lady.

The Rudder

It was a difficult lesson to realize that I wasn't in control of my life and never would be. This voice gave me absolutely no choice in the matter. Yet the voice was kind, with a warmth and caring that shone through its resolute message. It wasn't telling me this news so that I could change the course of events; the words were not put in those terms: "Do this instead," "If you listen to me everything will be fine," or "Avoid the man with the chronic nosebleed." No, the message stated, "Here are the facts." So why tell me this if I can't change it?

Was the voice trying to scare me? I was certainly scared. I could still hear the words echoing perfectly in my mind. It was as if the voice were trying to impart some difficult information as gently as it could, without possibility of error about the meaning of the words, in order that I might know the truth. It was like a doctor imparting the horrible news to a patient that he was terminally ill, and that while one couldn't say exactly how much longer he had to live, it was time for the patient to put his affairs in order and to make peace with his life. Apparently I needed time to prepare myself, and I needed to begin to reflect upon a greater, broader set of spiritual and philosophical possibilities than my current atheistic stance permitted.

If I were being prepared, how would this information help me? Would it help my future husband? Couldn't I just choose someone else who wouldn't meet an early death?

Since I still felt too young to marry and didn't know anyone I wished to marry, it seemed strange to refuse to marry "him." I didn't know "him" anyway. To say, "Whoever he is, I won't marry him. I'll marry some other whomever instead," made no sense. I wanted to say "NO!" but I felt like I didn't have anything or anyone to say "no" to.

I was scared, horrified, miserable, and felt myself to be without refuge. I didn't know anyone to whom I could tell this story who wouldn't think it silly, crazy, stupid, not just crazy, but truly insane, or all of the above. No one I knew would take such an experience seriously. My parents did not participate in any religious traditions or organizations, and so neither did I, but I wondered whether a church or a synagogue would be helpful in this matter anyway. Wouldn't a minister or rabbi think me silly or nuts as well? Didn't some groups characterize this sort of thing as the work of the "devil"? I had no one in whom to confide, so I didn't; I didn't say a word. I didn't begin to talk about what this voice had said for many, many years. Later I would think back to the time when I first learned of my fate on a beautiful afternoon so many years before, but then, that probably wasn't the beginning either. That giant wheel had been grinding its gears for time beyond counting.

The rest of the wedding reception was something of a blur. I drank punch and swung in the hammock. I played with the girl who had taken the bouquet, to whom I now felt a bond. I'm sure there's still a picture of us together somewhere, sitting and talking. She was just playing and being a kid, right? Anyway, she certainly couldn't stop my eventual marriage or change the destiny of my husband-to-be. Today I would say that she had graciously lent herself as an agent of fate on that day. The voice had a message for me, and I now know, or at least believe, that when the angels want to tell you something, they will.

The Morning Star

My earliest memory of a disembodied voice happened sometime around the age of seven. I was playing in my room by myself when a voice suddenly spoke to me with great authority, "You will be a writer when you grow up." It was a clear and definite statement, as I have discovered these messages tend to be. There was no room for discussion, argument, or the possibility of change. It was decided; it was a fact. I would be a writer. Along with the words came a sort of internal knowing accompanying the voiced command. This silent intuition let me know that I would write books and that I would be successful in my work. I accepted the message with the simplicity of a child, although at the time my play was filled with inventing my own languages and subjecting a few patient friends to lists of made-up vocabulary and accompanying grammar exercises for them to study as homework. How they tolerated me I will never know! I've met and befriended people as kind, patient, and lovely as those early friends since then, but I've not made better ones.

When I wasn't inventing brilliant new languages native to the northern climes in which I lived, yet mingled with the sounds of Eastern Europe from which my ancestors had fled, blended with tones of vowels and sentence structure from other lands, imagined by my childhood mind, I was designing houses with blocks and pieces of paneling and carpet. My parents didn't believe in buying plastic toys or ones that required batteries. Our third-hand black-and-white TV was kept in the closet, except when it was rolled out so that my brother and I (after we'd figured out that TV existed from the rumors of friends and began to lobby our parents) could watch "The Wonderful World of Disney" on Sunday evenings. Moon landings and courageous walks toward freedom were other occasions for this TV to make a brief appearance in our 1960s household. The rest of the time it was up to us to invent our own fun, so I used the carpet and paneling scraps my dad received for free from various businesses, the set of blocks he made me himself, and the love of words I absorbed from him ("Go get the dictionary" was a common refrain in our home), and I assembled houses and languages. I didn't dream of future professions or ever imagine myself as an adult at that age. I loved to read books, but it had never occurred to me that one day I too would try to write them. Books came from the library—another weekly ritual. Yet there I was, a future writer, wondering vaguely about who had just spoken to me. Despite being the sort of child who told her parents, most embarrassingly, just about everything, I told no one about what I had heard; I somehow knew that at that time this message was intended only for me.

As I grew older many more precognitive experiences, intuitions, and voices joined that first message in that unshared, little-looked-at area of my mind that I reserved for how I knew things about people and the world that I couldn't possibly know. I continued to keep the unseen promptings to myself. After all, both of my parents were psychotherapists, and before long I knew the official diagnosis of people who heard voices: stark raving mad! It wasn't until I reached my 20s that I began, tentatively, gradually, to try to talk to other people about the things that I was seeing and hearing, about information that would manifest, fully formed, in my mind. These experiences did not find a safe harbor in which to shelter among those I told about them. Mostly, I kept my mouth shut and worried silently about what was going on.

Yo, Ho, Ho and a Bottle of Rum

In middle school and high school the voice and invisible guidance usually left me alone, probably figuring that I had enough to deal with during adolescence without the added pressures of hearing voices and having visions, experiences that I felt guided to completely avoid talking about with my family and friends.

Once in a while, though, my guides would break their silence and pipe up with some piece of advice that they felt was too important not to share.

It was the 1970s, a time when the popular nutritional guidelines were shifting to advise a diet based on lots of carbohydrates and fiber, not much red meat, and an avoidance of fats such as butter and cream. People were being told, for example, to replace butter with margarine, a food-industry invented product that pumped trans fats and dangerous vegetable oils right to our arterial walls! That dietary advice, as we probably all know by now, was utterly wrong and horribly destructive, to heart health, to our colon, and to the waistline in particular. Americans started to get fatter. Then they got fatter still. It would take some years before the outrageous increases in diabetes, in cancers, and in dementia would become really evident, but the process was under way.

Like many people of that time, I tried to eat a more vegetarian diet. I became ill quite quickly, slowed down by low energy and anemia. As I followed my doctor's advice to start eating red meat and other animal proteins again, my guides couldn't help chiming in, "You have to eat meat. It's really important. Don't try to be a vegetarian."

This advice might seem pointless to some and false to others, but I've heard it repeated over the years, from time to time, when I thought I might try switching to a more plant-based diet.

When I have followed the guidance to eat animal protein, I've become slimmer. When I haven't listened, I've gained weight and become anemic.

While my guides were insisting that I eat plenty of meat, they were also telling me not to smoke.

"Look at the adults around you who smoke. What do they all have in common?"

"They're all trying to quit smoking," I replied silently to whomever was instructing me.

"How are they doing with quitting?" the voice inquired.

"Some of them have succeeded, but a lot of people are still struggling, still addicted to smoking."

"Do you know anyone who smokes cigarettes who would like to continue smoking them? Not teenagers. Grown-ups."

"No. They all want to quit."

"Do you think that you would have an easier time quitting smoking, if you started, than other people?"

"No. Why would it be easier for me?"

"Exactly."

My guides at times had the charm and personality of a schoolmarm, hair wrenched back from the face in a tight bun, glasses sliding down the nose as they peered at me below, but I couldn't fault their logic.

The Eye of the Storm

I was driving down the road while trying to avoid hitting or being hit by one car in particular whose driver seemed hell-bent on causing an accident as he played games with the other drivers by weaving in and out of traffic and speeding up and slowing down; I thought to myself, "What in the world is he thinking!"

Not as alone in the car as I had thought myself to be, I heard, "I don't know. I never studied child psychology."

Okay. So my guides could have a sense of humor too. I started laughing. The fully-grown man driving erratically and irresponsibly in traffic was acting like a three-year-old having a temper tantrum. Unfortunately, he was also driving 1,000 pounds of machinery, erratically, down the road. Throwing a tantrum would have been unseemly enough in an adult, but rather than lying on the floor, yelling with flailing limbs, he was lurching a large chunk of metal to and fro.

Now, though, instead of continuing to get angry, I found the whole situation funny. The driver was acting like a spoiled child who hadn't gotten his way, angry at the world for some reason or other and actively seeking to make other people suffer, pay, even, for his personal pain and perhaps rather complicated life.

I can still get annoyed with other drivers who I believe are breaking the unspoken social contract that I think everyone who drives should engage in: to help everyone on the road stay safe. That day, however, marked an early experience in learning to let go of other people's problems and craziness rather than internalizing them, rather than trying to argue with them, understand them, or change them. Instead, I was shown that I should notice what's going on, stay detached, and keep a safe driving distance, whether in a car or not.

It's been a difficult lesson for me to fully absorb, and I continue to be presented with opportunities to master the concept that I am responsible for healing myself, for becoming a kinder and gentler and more helpful human being, and yet I have no responsibility to try to fix the bad behavior of others.

I'm often asked to pray for others, and I do pray for myself, for family and friends, and for the world as a whole–daily. Meanwhile, it has been made clear to me that in this lifetime it is my job to clear my own drama from my lunchroom tray and not worry about the cafeteria food fight starting up at a neighboring table.

Beached

Before the start of my senior year of high school, I went with my friend and her family to the seaside and had a great time. She and I both got sunburned, but my sunburn was definitely worse. School began and I found that I wasn't able to wear a bra–my skin had blistered around my shoulders and upper chest and even bending or turning my upper body could be very painful. I didn't want to broadcast too much personal detail to my classmates, so my solution was to wear a fairly form-fitting T-shirt covered by a loose over-shirt. I might have been a bit warm that early September, but I maintained some privacy.

A real problem arose, though, when I spoke with the coach about not being able to play field hockey for a couple of weeks.

"I can't wear a bra, and it hurts when I move, especially if I twist or raise my arms. I definitely can't run or swing a stick yet."

Practice was starting, and I couldn't participate. The coach promptly dropped me from the team. I was incredulous. This wasn't varsity. This wasn't even the junior varsity team. I was on the third string, a team, and we were a team that played games against other schools, really we were, a team that was made up of girls who either, as freshmen and sophomores, just hadn't made the more accomplished teams yet, or, like me, a senior, just liked to run around and hit the ball, but didn't actually care anything about winning. This progressive school's philosophy was about tolerance and inclusion long before they became popularized values, but perhaps the coach believed in the "No pain, no gain" motto, an idea I've always found particularly foolhardy. Work hard? Check. Contribute to society? All for it. Suffer? Why would someone want to do that if it could be avoided? But that's me.

Did the team members really care if we won or lost? Many of my teammates probably didn't. Clearly, the coach did, although how I would get significantly better or worse at the game if I missed a couple of weeks of practice, I didn't know. Perhaps I had demonstrated negligence by allowing myself to get so badly burned. Maybe the coach just finally had an excuse to drop me from the team.

I'm not saying that everyone was like me, a player who had never actually learned all of the rules of the game, even after playing it for four years, but it seemed like a pretty relaxed group and game. We were out to have fun. We'd practice, we'd try to win when we played, but we didn't really care if we lost. We chatted in the locker room as we changed, joked on the bus as we headed to our games; we were a friendly bunch.

"Off-sides? I probably should know what that is by now. Is it important for a full-back to know what that means? Should I ask someone to explain it to me again?"

It was about sportsmanship, not the score, I reasoned. That had been my impression, anyway.

I was kicked off the team, such as it was, and allowed to let my horrible burns heal as they might. There was a problem, though. Field hockey was "my sport." I mean that in the loosest, vaguest way possible. I didn't have a sport, but since all students were required to have a sport, I'd picked field hockey. I was terrible at basketball and lacrosse didn't appeal. Running hurt, so track was out. Tennis, anyone? Not sure why I didn't do that. Probably because the other girls were really good and I wasn't. There wasn't really anything else left, so field hockey it was. I tried hard in the moment, but deep down, I couldn't have cared less about the sport. However, it was a school requirement to participate in at least one sport per year; one couldn't graduate without it.

"I should learn life-saving." The thought came to me unbidden. It was emphatic as well, a trait of certain signs and directives that later I would come to recognize as important and learn to pay attention to. I was still pretty new at following guidance, but the directive made sense. I explained the problem and possible solution to my parents, and they agreed to let me sign up for life-saving lessons at the Y, paying for them, and allowing me to borrow the car so I could get back and forth.

I only completed Junior Life-Saving, my diving not being up to the Senior Life-Saving level, but it felt like enough. The voices were satisfied and offered no further comment on the issue. Meanwhile, I'd completed the necessary physical education hours for school. Life-saving classes turned out to be fun and I learned a lot, finishing up in plenty of time to have the sports credits needed for graduation.

After graduation I met up with my mother's family for a vacation, staying with my aunt, a wonderful lady I'd always thought of as my second mother. I was at the beach, but it was fairly empty, many people at the resort choosing to take a rest in their nearby rooms during the heat of the day or off doing other non-beach sorts of things. My one cousin and I decided to go swimming together and headed to the raft moored a ways out. We'd swum together before and she was a competent, if not a great, swimmer. What I hadn't realized is that this cousin, who had been ill since childhood, was perhaps now doing rather worse. We got to the raft easily and hung out on and around it for a while. As we started back to shore for some reason she began to panic; she stopped swimming and began to flail.

Unfazed, I zoomed over to her, held on to her upper arm, and described a fun way to swim to shore with me on my back and with her lying on top of my stomach and kicking her legs if she felt like it. I was the big sister-cousin, and she trusted me. This isn't a life-saving technique to use under many conditions. If the person you're trying to help is really freaking out, you could easily both go down. However, it's the one that I felt guided to use, perhaps in part because it seemed like a game and gave her a role and some sense of control. She relaxed a bit and kicked her legs as she hung on to my body, laying her head on my chest. I managed to steer her back to shallow water a short time later.

"I just saved her life," I realized.

Yes, she always had someone with her when swimming, but after that event we only swam with her where our feet could touch the bottom.

Did my guides lead me to be an idiot and get a really bad sunburn, a bit of a feat because I generally found sun-bathing boring and used a lot of sun screen when I did venture out under the sun's rays? Did my angels make the coach decide that she should "fire" my ass rather than let me rejoin the team in a couple of weeks?

I don't know, but I do know that the idea of life-saving classes came to me, seemingly out of nowhere, and that I understood that I had to make time for them and take them. I needed the credits, and there weren't any other options available. Spirit guided me to acquire the skills and confidence to help out when and how it would soon be needed. I've never had to use this skill set in all of the years since that day, but I definitely relied on them then. Apparently angels can use anything, even a sunburn, for their purposes.

My cousin died not so long ago, after many years of illness. I got to see her and talk to her, even if she wasn't able to respond, before she made the ultimate journey, time at last for her to reach the final shore.

If I had been her I might have wanted to move on a bit sooner, but then again, maybe not. I've learned to trust in God's timing and plan. We see so little and understand even less. Better to have Spirit prepare us and lead us instead. We continuously teach each other, it seems, including in death.

The Shallows

As I got closer to heading to college, my guides, more than once, reminded me that I was not supposed to do drugs, including alcohol. I still tried drinking a bit at times, but by early in my freshman year of college they told me to stop, to really stop with only small, rare exceptions being made. Once in a while I'd get the "all clear" signal and could have a drink with friends, but not often.

I had gotten a waitressing job in a bar. Although this establishment sold some food like pizza as well as booze, people came there primarily to drink, perhaps with a calzone on the side.

I hadn't seen the pattern that was to emerge in my working life yet, but I didn't have the proper credentials for my job–never have, perhaps never will. I guess there aren't proper credentials if one wants to be a psychic or intuitive or whatever one might call it, but I needed an emergency license when I first taught school, and the rules have had to be bent, at least somewhat, for many of the jobs I've had over the years. The issue at the bar, had it ever come up, was that I was too young to legally serve the clientele all that they might order. Oh well. I looked older.

In my job I watched table after table of customers get drunk. It was sad. It was a fun job in many ways because I met and talked to a lot of people and I got good tips, but watching the excessive consumption of alcohol, night after night, mostly just made me feel sorry for the people I served.

I always shared all of the tips I earned with my fellow servers at the end of the night so that we could divvy them up equally, as we had agreed to do. I sensed that no one else but me put all of the tips they'd earned into the pot. I could feel the truth of that intuition, but I put all of my tips into the jar at the end of the night anyway. I thought of sneaking away some of my tips into a pocket during the evening, but the feeling I got when I considered that idea was unpleasant and seemed wrong, so I never did. I was the only college student among career servers. I'd say that they needed the money more than I did, but I know that for many of them their earnings found their way up their noses–it was now the 80's, after all, and cocaine was a popular and expensive drug. I shared all my tips, not to support someone in the stupidity of a drug habit but because that was our agreement and I was going to follow through with it whether anyone else did or not. Spirit demanded a high degree of integrity from me regardless of what others thought or did, and the angels pulled me forward on this path as well, step by step.

"Watch other people and try to see the mistakes they're making and learn from them. You don't have to make all the mistakes yourself."

"What do you mean?"

"You're going to make plenty of mistakes in this lifetime. It comes with the territory. However, there are lots of mistakes you can avoid if you pay attention. Save yourself some of the pain and hardship that comes with living a human life. Do yourself a favor and avoid some of the most common and foolhardy pitfalls," I was advised.

"Some books you're going to have to read yourself,"

the explanation continued, "but sometimes it's enough just to understand the plotline. Sometimes you can listen to the book report, not read the entire tome. Maybe you can skim the CliffNotes without having to read the collected works of a particular author."

"Author?"

"Problem. We're using metaphor here. Some mistakes are silly, and the science about the dangers of smoking cigarettes has been well-known for some time. Both of your parents had to work hard to quit smoking. Learn from their example. Not the 'start smoking and then having to quit part,' the mistake of beginning a habit that you already know is bad for you, is expensive, and harms your health–that part."

"Some of the people around you drink too much, some of them are becoming alcoholics or problem drinkers while others are already there. Some people spend a lot of their money, time, and brain cells pursuing drug use. How many of them do you think will kick these unhealthy and destructive lifestyles? When? Before they cause problems for themselves and their family? Before it hurts their marriage? Before they run into problems at work? Many people will continue these patterns for the rest of their lives."

"For those who take the steps to get clean or sober, will it be easy or difficult? How about skimming the chapter titles for the main points and then skipping ahead through the book? What about reading the ending first? Take the moral of the story and learn from it. You don't have to read a book if you've already learned what it has to teach you."

"Got it."

When I say, "got it," I mean that I got it, got this lesson without having to make the mistakes in terms of drugs and alcohol. Those were not pitfalls for me. However, the rest of my life probably wasn't any smoother than anyone else's. Poor choices, wrong turns, and acting the fool are all a part of my repertoire.

Circe, The False Enchantress

At the end of the night everyone who worked at the bar was offered a free drink, our choice of a shot or a beer or whatever, before heading home. By this time it was early in the morning. The thought that I might have a class in a little while was not what kept me from accepting that drink. I didn't want to think of drinking as some kind of reward. I didn't want to join the aspect of my culture that glorified drinking, especially the drinking of a lot of alcohol, as somehow cool or sexy. I drank little-to-none from that time on, sometimes going a few years at a time without a sip of alcohol. At age 40 I heard, "You can drink now."

I guess I'm slow to mature. Since then, I'll have a glass of wine or a beer once in a while, and a couple of glasses of wine with a special dinner or at a party. That feels like enough.

My friends drank, though, and some of them drank a lot and often. Many of my friends in college did drugs on a regular basis. I found that some of the most interesting, weird, independent thinkers were taking drugs. They were great people, but those choices didn't appeal to me. I'd rather eat cookies any day–a habit with its own pitfalls, of course, but one that my angels didn't seem to take an interest in.

I developed a strategy to go out early. I'd meet up with friends in a bar or at a party, but I'd arrive and leave early, getting some social time in without the boozing. I'd be one of the first people at a party, not showing up "fashionably late" but instead at the time I'd been told the party was set to start. If people seemed to be getting drunk, I knew that was my exit cue. If there was good music I might stay a while longer and dance. I decided that I wanted to be able to have fun yet without social awkwardness, without needing to enter into some kind of altered state through alcohol or pot or whatever other people were doing. I decided that I would be really sociable, talk to lots of people, and dance around like an idiot, but without the social lubricant provided by mind-altering substances so popular among many of my peers.

More than once, as I flailed and boogied on the dance floor, I heard someone comment along the lines of, "What's she on?"

"Nothing. She's like that stone cold sober."

"Wow. She seems drunk."

"I know, but she's not. She's just like that."

I hovered in the teetotaler range until I got the "all clear" signal as I entered middle age. I was now allowed to have a drink or two if I wanted. I guess the danger of me turning into an alcoholic had passed at last.

"I started drinking in my 40s," I tell people. I get the strangest looks.

The Wine-Dark Sea

Why was I warned more about alcohol and other kinds of drugs more than I was about making most other kinds of mistakes in life? Why am I sometimes still guided not to have a glass of wine, even with a steak with which it would pair perfectly? Why do I often receive the suggestion to meet a friend for a walk or a cup of tea rather than for a drink in town?

I think that I was told to steer clear of drugs, including anti-depressants while I was really depressed during my sophomore year of college, because one of my biggest lessons in this lifetime has been about learning to be present for life, even if it's really uncomfortable, even if I would prefer to engage in some kind of escape mechanism. Rather than masking a problem, I'm asked to acknowledge and feel it before shifting or working to release it. Rather than covering up a symptom, I was invited to unmask the deeper issues and dis-ease operating under the surface.

I'm not saying that other people shouldn't take anti-depressants when they need them–of course they should. In my case, though, I've usually been asked to avoid medications, whether to help me sleep, for allergies, or for coping with life's woes and turmoil.

The lesson in life, our main task as human beings, and it's not just my lesson, is to learn how to face the moment with open eyes, an open mind, and a ready heart. So, even if we need to take an allergy pill, we can also meditate every day. Even if we need to take something to help relieve depression or anxiety, we can also read spiritual and self-help books to deepen our understanding of our patterns and unhelpful habits of mind.

Daily life presents so many challenges, from the unkind words and actions of others to traffic jams, long lines at the grocery store, and listening to an endless automated phone system only to then be put on hold as soon as a human being answers. Chores need doing, bills demand to be paid, disagreements arise, people sometimes get sick, and on and on. The daily joys are mixed with obstacles and difficulties. Even when on vacation we can't fully escape our troubles, our unhappy thoughts and negative emotions intruding even into peaceful landscapes– or others insist on inflicting their emotional upheaval on us.

Modern life is bursting with opportunities to avoid our feelings, other people, and even the world itself. TV can function as a babysitter for adults who can't handle any further interaction or responsibilities when they return home from work, perhaps exhausted and emotionally depleted. The Internet, gaming, gambling, pornography, constant texting, and various other forms of media and technology, to write a very short list, can function as avoidance mechanisms through which to exit one's life while seemingly still being present.

The Internet can be a useful tool for learning and work, or it can become a rabbit hole into which one can fall until it's time for bed. Texting and social media, while fun and often useful, can easily be overused.

Why do we sink ourselves into one distraction after another? Probably because otherwise we will have to sit with ourselves, with our rambling and often destructive, thoughts, and simply be. We'd have to face our uncomfortable emotions, the mistakes of our past, and our turbulent thoughts. Instead, we might decide that it's time to take up meditation, yoga, or tai chi, and to engage in grounding, centering practices that will help us chart a course into calmer waters.

Our culture encourages us to constantly do, to be on the move, and to accomplish more and more. The deeper path, the one that leads to greater wisdom, peace, and contentment, however, requires us to be present for our lives, to really notice the moment, and to listen within.

My guides have often instructed me to work hard, even really hard. When I taught I would spend countless hours researching and preparing each course, take on extra classes, and cover the classes, sometimes for entire semesters, for sick colleagues. I've often carried a second job in addition to the long hours required by my full-time job, and once in a while I've had a full-time job plus two part-time jobs. And I'm not a slacker at work–I give it my all–so much so that I've often been made fun of by colleagues who tell me I work too much, that I'm a workaholic. Actually, I love to work. By working you make money, learn new things, interact with people, and have the opportunity to stretch and grow as a human being every single day.

At the same time as I've been guided to work hard, my guides have been trying to teach me to become more and more conscious and aware, to take time every day to sit quietly in stillness, to breathe more deeply, to listen to others and to the world more attentively, and not just to pray, but to receive the answers and guidance offered in response.

I've been told to drink very little or not at all for much of my life because Spirit doesn't want me to miss the show. I've got a human lifetime to live–I'm not supposed to be checked out and befuddled. Instead, I'm supposed to be paying attention. I'm asked to focus on each moment, no matter how unpleasant or uncomfortable, and to just stay with it, allowing it to be. It's hard to force myself to be present, but it has led to the greatest growth I've experienced.

As I've often thought, when I get to the end of this lifetime and I'm asked to give an accounting of myself and of how I used my time, I don't want to be have to say, "What? You mean I was supposed to be paying attention?"

A Parrot on One's Shoulder

I had been finding it difficult to concentrate in college, and this revelation, this voice telling me that I would lose my first husband, didn't help at all. I hadn't known what to study before and had been asking myself some tricky "meaning of life" questions for a while. I guess that when you start asking, eventually something will come along to join the inquiry, turning soliloquy into dialogue.

Me: "Why am I here? What does it all mean? What does studying this stuff have to do with real life? Are we destined to die alone, disintegrating into the void? Blah, blah, blah, and on and on and on…for years."

A disembodied voice: "The first one will be taken from you."

Me: "What? What do you mean? There's something listening to all this endless drivel? Who in the world would have the patience for that? If you're willing to speak to me at all, why stop? How about a few more sentences, for clarity's sake? What's with the dead husband prophecy?"

Disembodied voice: Total and utter silence.

Batten Down the Hatches

In the spring of my freshman year of college, my best friend Pam and I entered the housing lottery to try to get a room in the most coveted dorm at the college. Our numbers were pretty low, mine especially, but we squeaked in, our number in the lottery awarding us a specific, small double room. We stopped by the room to see where we'd be living the next year and to meet the people living there now. It must have been one of the rooms allocated to sophomores every year because the guy who answered the door was in his second year. We explained to him, excitedly, that we were going to be living there next year.

"You got this room? Oh no. That's not good. My roommate had to leave school. Every year the student who sleeps on this side of the room goes crazy or drops out," he explained, pointing to the right side of the room as we looked through the door. "It happened last year and the year before that too. I don't know how far back it goes, but it happens every year."

"I'll take that side," I said, pointing at the doomed side of the room.

"Okay." I think that Pam thought that what the guy was saying was all silliness and superstition. There couldn't possibly be any truth or reality to it. I wasn't sure what to make of what he was saying either, but I wasn't able to completely dismiss it. Still reluctant to follow the signs offered, I agreed to move into that dorm room the next year anyway and even to berth in the section for which storms were forecast.

Knowing what I know now, I would never have agreed to take that room at all, not any part of it. Actually, what I would have done, had I understood then what I now know how to do, would be to read the energy of the room. If I'd encountered an inhabiting spirit, I would have completely cleared the room of the soul who still occupied it. Of course, I didn't understand any of that then. I didn't know that there really are such things as ghosts, let alone mean-spirited ones, and I certainly had no idea how to safely clear them when they were present.

What is a ghost? I now believe in ghosts, but I definitely don't like them or find them cute or intriguing. A "ghost" is just someone who has died but has not crossed into the Light. When one enters the Light, one receives a light body that heals and completely replaces the physical one left behind. If one sticks around one's old life as a ghost, lurking around the people and places one knew while alive, one still carries the heavy and ineffective previous body, including all injuries and illnesses that it experienced during that lifetime.

Lugging an aged, wounded, decaying, or incomplete "body" around can be very painful. In addition, in that undead state the ghost doesn't have access to energy of its own because it can't eat or drink or rest or renew itself in any way. Instead, it draws energy from the people it haunts and the places it inhabits, often making its former friends, family, and even strangers who stay in that house, hotel room or, in this case, dorm room, drained, dispirited, sick, and possibly even ill to the point of losing one's life. The longer one is exposed to the ghost, the more severely impacted one will be. Even the kindest, friendliest person (this happens less frequently) who has died but not entered the Light will negatively impact the people and places it visits and will leave them tired, depressed, confused, and harm their health, both physical and emotional.

Now I understand that my side of the dorm room had once been occupied by someone who had killed himself while he was a student; like many suicides, he had never crossed into the Light. This soul, who had not yet departed the physical realm, had continued to torment, every single year since his death, whoever was living on "his" side of the room.

Today I would remove any ghosts I encountered, but at that time I didn't understand what was going on and I certainly didn't possess the skill set to effectively neutralize the issue. At some point that tortured soul made his way, finally, into the Light. I'm not the one who helped him cross over. Maybe the angels eventually convinced him to return to the Light. Maybe a priest with entity-ridding expertise was called in. At the time, though, the guy who invisibly occupied that room was incredibly angry, just as he had been prior to taking his own life.

Moving beyond the body, from the physical to the spiritual plane, is no guarantee of enlightenment or even of greater understanding, kindness, or compassion. Over the years I've encountered many, many departed souls, both those in the Light and ones who continued to linger around their former lives. What I've discovered is that the state of mind or level of understanding and awareness one is in when one departs an earthly lifetime is the same state of mind or degree of consciousness one has a moment later in "death." Yes, when one enters the Light one has access to much greater truth, love, and insight, but one isn't always ready to receive it, even then. We head to the Light when we pass away and from there we have the opportunity to continue on our journey, gaining new wisdom and gradually moving upwards into higher and higher realms of consciousness, peace, joy, and service.

I didn't understand any of that as I stood there, a rather lost and confused 18-year-old. I didn't understand how serious a situation it was that we were entering nor how badly I would fare by deciding to take the brunt of whatever was coming our way when Pam and I moved into that room the following term.

Hard Tack and Salt Pork

Sophomore year began, and I became more and more depressed. It was harder and harder for me to get up on time for classes in the morning. Before long, it was hard for me to get out of bed at all. There were days when I probably only got up to eat and use the bathroom.

Pam told me that I was having a nervous breakdown. I didn't know what a nervous breakdown was, but that wasn't what I thought was happening. I couldn't name what was happening, couldn't really explain it or talk about it to anyone, but my mood was dark, I felt sad for no reason I could explain, and I felt like a weight was pressing down on me, rather literally, much of the time. I found it almost impossible to concentrate and fell behind, quickly, in my studies. I broke up with my boyfriend, a really nice guy, because I decided that it would be better if I were alone. It was a bleak time.

Early in the school year the voice, not that of my guides, of course, but the one that had found its way into my head since I'd moved into this dorm room, told me, "You might not have kids. Maybe you will, but you might not. There's a pretty good chance you won't have kids in this lifetime."

I was horrified. I had never heard or seen anything bad before when receiving information from beyond myself. I was planning on having kids. I was counting on it. Now, suddenly, I was hearing that I really might not get to have kids.

Where was this information coming from? Why was I being told this? The sadness that I'd been feeling, continuously, since moving into this new room increased. Who could I possibly tell about what I was hearing? For the first time in my life I was hearing a hostile voice, one that didn't wish me well. One, in fact, that seemed to want to hurt me, that wanted to cause me pain.

I lay there listening to Joni Mitchell records, which, although the lady has talent beyond measure, certainly added to my depression. Thoughts of suicide began to impinge upon my mind. I'd not entertained those thoughts before, not even in high school, a time when many kids, no matter how briefly, have those sorts of ideas flit across their mind. Now the idea of suicide badgered me daily. I argued with it and told those thoughts to go away. I didn't understand that what I was actually trying to do was to make the dead guy with those thoughts go away and leave me alone. I didn't know what I was doing or to whom I was really speaking, so I wasn't the least bit successful at shutting up that awful noise.

Pam and I had an unhappy ghost in the room, and he was attaching himself to both of our energy fields, although much more to mine since I was in "his" space, using "his" desk and occupying "his" bed, which he hadn't left and didn't think he was done with yet. I was the interloper. I was in his way. His horrible thoughts overwhelmed me, dragging me further and further downwards. I went to a therapist at the school for a while until I realized that not only was she not helping me, she was making things worse. At least I had the sense not to tell her about the external voices that were attacking me on a daily basis–I might have ended up with the "crazy" diagnosis of some of the other former inhabitants of that dorm room.

I tried to study but it was like trying to wade upstream, over rocks, in a swiftly flowing river. I talked to my parents about the hard time I was having studying and going to class; they told me to try harder and to study more. That advice might have made sense under normal circumstances, but these were not normal circumstances.

I wanted, desperately, to leave school, but my parents wouldn't let me. Really, what I wanted, on an intuitive level, was to get the hell away from the entity that was trying to take me over. I didn't understand what was going on, fortunately, because I probably would have been institutionalized if I'd understood and then tried to explain my situation to someone. I was in a bad place and I had no one to help me, at least not effectively or successfully. Sure, it might have looked like a nervous breakdown, but that was not what was going on. I was under attack by a dark and unquiet soul. I was being continually harassed by the undead, a sort of zombie as a rent-free roommate.

I never pursued the idea of suicide in any way, no matter how constantly I had the idea shoved at me. "No!" I would yell back at the idea in my head. "Absolutely not! I refuse!"

Finally, I made a promise to myself that I never, ever, under any circumstances, no matter what I went through and no matter what happened to me or in my life, would I agree to kill myself. Suicide was not an option. It was completely off the table. Period.

I had told that voice to stop and to go away from the very beginning, but when I made that profound promise to myself, when I made that unwavering pact, something greater than myself must have said, "That's it. That's done. She is never going to kill herself. You don't get to say that any more."

Anchors Aweigh

The dead kid was still around, his energy weighing heavily on and around me, but at least his voice had been largely silenced. I began to recover a bit, although not quickly enough to save my grades. My mind did begin to clear, though, and I formed a plan. No matter what my parents said, I was going to leave school for a year.

My parents were completely against me leaving school, although what they were afraid of, I don't know. I loved school. I loved to read books, to study, and to learn new things. I was a committed nerd. That wasn't about to change. I just needed to get away for a while. I needed to think my own thoughts, not the crazy thoughts of the disturbed undead! Without understanding the details, I knew that I needed to learn to think more deeply for myself. In school I was learning to echo the thoughts of other people, great writers and thinkers from the past. That was all very interesting, but I needed to try out some thoughts of my own for a while.

Fortunately, I had saved some money, so I was able to buy a one-way plane ticket to Europe and a month-long Eurail pass to travel by train in an unrestricted way. For my birthday my parents bought me a backpack and a Swiss Army knife. Thanks for the knife, Dad and Mom! It will come in handier than you might realize.

I flew to Luxembourg where I had a friend, visited for a few days, and then began getting on and off trains, staying in youth hostels as I went. I sent post cards home regularly and once in a while made a brief, but expensive phone call to the States to let them know I was alive and well.

I started my Eurail trip in Belgium and realized that first night in the youth hostel in Brussels that I needed to get over my shyness, and that I needed to do so immediately. I walked over to some other women in my dorm who were talking to each other, introduced myself, joined the conversation, and never looked back.

I felt great. I was finally myself again. My mind cleared from its pain and fog. My thoughts were once again my own.

At one point in my travels, during one of our quick chats, my father asked me if I'd ever seen a map of Europe. I assured him that I even owned one and carried it about in my backpack and studied it regularly.

"Why are you criss-crossing Europe, going back and forth across countries?"

I tried to explain how I chose where to go next. "I go to the train station and look at the board to see which trains are leaving soon and where they're headed. If I'm saving money, I pick an overnight train. Sometimes I just jump on the next train leaving the station and go wherever it takes me."

To my highly left-brained planner of a father, that approach made no sense. He would just laugh and say, "Really, I don't think she knows how to read a map!"

I was good at reading maps, actually, taught from a young age by my father who was something of an expert when it came to maps. He had taught me to love them too.

I found them strangely fascinating, full of the unknown, of interesting places to discover tucked away here and there, of mystery and possibilities. I enjoyed looking over the map, of noticing where Switzerland connected to Italy, where Italy brushed sides with France. It was all great fun. I just wasn't going to let a map tell me where to go next. In my mind I was leaving it all to chance and whim. Looking back at my "process," I think I was enjoying feeling free again after the constant mental and emotional oppression by the troubled ghost during the previous school year. I was free to think and do as I pleased, and it was such a relief. I also think that I was beginning to practice living from a sort of flow state in which the next step to take appeared, and then the next and the next. It's a form of faith to trust that things will work out and that whatever I needed to do or say or take care of next would show itself to me when that moment appeared.

I took this trip many years ago, but after purchasing my month-long train ticket, I managed to live on $11.50 per day, including meals and lodging. To save money I walked almost everywhere rather than taking busses or subways. I usually logged 20-25 miles a day, some of it with my backpack. I bought food at grocery stores and mostly ate my bread, cheese, and salami picnic style as I went along. On one really broke day I had a banana sandwich for lunch. I was pretty determined to stay within budget, so if I went to a museum I just had to economize in other ways. I'm not complaining; the trip taught me so much, and I was well aware, both then and now, that I am fortunate and blessed in ways beyond counting. I enjoyed being self-reliant and I rejoiced in the sense of freedom and independence I felt after a school-year spent dueling it out with a hostile and relentless, yet disembodied, entity.

I bought nothing—no souvenirs or clothes or anything else. I was there to see Europe, and by walking around towns and cities on foot I got to know some of the places I visited quite well. It was a cathartic and healing trek.

Port of Call

My Eurail pass ended as I arrived in my destination country–let's call it Spain. A friend picked me up at the train station, saying nothing at all about my impossibly hairy legs–my defense strategy against unwanted amorous attention. It had kept everyone away, actually, who harbored any romantic ideas. That had been part of my freedom. No dating and no hassles.

I placed an ad in the newspaper offering my services as an English tutor. I found a couple of jobs teaching English in schools as well.

If my father had seen where the schools were located and the different houses I would go to for tutoring, he would have inquired as to whether or not I had ever seen a map of that town, either. I just took whatever jobs were offered, and I was offered enough to keep me busy more than full time as I crossed back and forth around the city and its immediate suburbs.

As luck would have it, some or all of the public transportation was on strike that year, individually or together, so I walked and walked and walked from one job to the next. During one particularly difficult period, the military actually put its jeeps into action to help people get around.

The route home from my Friday evening school, with two buses, or no buses, depending, took me past a couple of movie theaters. I would notice what was playing on my way to work and often would hop off the bus to catch a flick on the way home.

I was working hard, but I was free and independent and steadily healing my beleaguered mind and tired spirit.

The room I shared with a roommate contained a copy of Viktor Frankl's book, *Man's Search for Meaning*, about his years spent surviving, just barely, in concentration camps during World War Two; I read that short, inspiring volume through twice. Dr. Frankl spoke of how we can find meaning in life no matter how much grief and loss we experience, no matter how miserable our circumstances might seem, or how much pain and suffering we endure.

As he demonstrated under the worst possible circumstances, if we decide to, we can find meaning in our lives in each and every moment, and if we do that, we will always be free in our hearts. His powerful message spoke to my core and permanently changed me. He would never have written, or have been able to write, that beautiful book without having gone through such tremendous pain and loss. He had concluded that even his suffering had purpose and meaning. Why not mine then, however trivial my suffering by comparison? Why not mine as well? Why not yours and everyone else's?

It's not about turning lemons into lemonade. That works in some situations, but sometimes there don't even seem to be any lemons lurking about. Instead, what Frankl did was more radical–he created hope and meaning and purpose out of the thin air of his cold, starving, and grieving time spent in camps, surrounded by gruesome behavior and a stream of death. He saw the worst of which humans are capable, and it was truly awful, yet he found truth and wisdom hiding in its midst.

Taking On Water

After working in Spain for a year, I returned to the United States to continue my studies, ready to refocus now that it had been a full year since the unwanted voice's constant harassment and disparagement in my old dorm room. I'd taught English successfully, learned a lot, and had developed as a teacher. Now it was time to finish school.

I hadn't been back in the U.S. long at all when I attended Gabrielle's wedding and heard the voice informing me that my first husband would die. Here I was, back on my feet again, and I was already having the ground beneath me heave and toss, trying to find my balance on choppy seas.

I enjoyed most of the rest of my classes, and I took many, many of them–far more than I needed to graduate– but there was always a little part of me that was wary, that was nervous about what I'd see or hear next. I knew I had hard times ahead, as we all surely do, but I had just turned 21, younger than some, perhaps, to be besieged with thoughts of death and widowhood.

Finally, all I had left to finish in order to receive my degree were a couple of incomplete grades. I had to write a long paper for two classes and then I'd be done. I needed a full-time job to pay my bills.

My job interview at a science lab went something like this:

"So what is your background in Chemistry?"

"None, except for the class I had in high school."

"So you have a background in Biology?"

"Just high school Biology."

"Oh. Well have you worked in a lab before?"

"No, I've never worked in a lab."

"Well, how are you at computers?"

"I've never even touched one before." This was the 1980s, so that wasn't nearly as strange as it might sound to a reader today.

"Could you start next week?"

"Yes."

So I began to work in a cancer research lab and was therefore weirdly positioned when my brother was diagnosed with that frightening disease.

All Hands On Deck

After receiving the news of his cancer diagnosis from my parents, I immediately called my boss to explain that I'd have to miss a couple of days of work. Then I began to frantically pack up some things, getting ready to drive to where my brother was in a hospital room, several states away, sitting with our parents who had just arrived by his side. His surgery was scheduled for nine the next morning.

I packed some clothes, still stunned by the news I'd received, and waited impatiently to greet and give keys to some friends who had flown in from Europe, were arriving shortly, and were going to stay in my place, although while I was gone, it now turned out.

The friends arrived, were greeted, quick explanations were offered for my absence, the keys were handed over, and I jumped into the car.

I'm a cautious driver, so I was surprised to hear a voice telling me to go faster.

"His surgery isn't scheduled until nine. I have time to get there before his surgery," I explained to the voice telling me to speed.

"Go faster!"

I sped up somewhat, and in response to further promptings, again a bit more. The voice urged me to driver faster the entire way as I struggled against my fear of speeding tickets and my reluctance to go too fast. Hours later I neared the hospital, driving full out. If there had been someone watching (a live human being, that is) they probably would have thought I was being chased. If there had been police nearby, I would have gotten one hell of a ticket, but conveniently there weren't any police around just as I hadn't seen a single cop once during all of the hours of my drive. They'd been cleared from my path, I suppose, as I'd sped across state lines.

I jumped out of the car, slamming the door behind me, ran into the hospital, explained breathlessly who I needed to see to the woman at the information desk, and then grabbed an elevator and ran to his room. His room was empty.

"Where's my brother? Where did he go?" I demanded at the nurses' station.

"Oh, they decided to take him in early." They gave me directions to the floor where he'd been taken. Once I'd careened to that nurses' station, they told me that I needed to go around a corner and down a hall and make another turn, and that I'd see him in front of the doors there. If I didn't see him there, that meant he'd already been taken in for surgery. I was told that I was not allowed to go through the doors to the surgical theater. That was logical. That's not what happened.

I zoomed around the corner and down the hallway. He wasn't outside the door.

"Fuck it!" I decided as I pushed my way into the surgical room where he lay, staring at the door I'd just come through as if willing me to appear. Our parents stood at his side.

"I knew you'd make it," he told me. "I knew you'd get here in time."

I just held his hand as I reassured him that I was there, that he was going to be okay, that I was with him, and that he didn't need to worry.

A few minutes later my parents and I were ushered outside to the waiting room to stare blankly at walls, to cry, to wait.

After some time the surgeon came out to tell us that my brother was doing well and that he thought they'd gotten all of the cancer.

The doctor left and my mother broke down. As she cried in my arms I said the words, "It's going to be okay, Mom. It's all going to be okay. It's going to be a hard year, and he's going to need more surgeries, but he will come through it all fine."

She looked at me, disbelief in her eyes as she started to yell at me, to tell me that I knew and understood nothing, that I didn't know what he was going through, and that I couldn't possibly predict what was coming. This was cancer!

I tried to just stay there holding her, supportive, listening to her somehow blaming me for events. I was too stunned, though, to say much. That was the first time in my life that I'd opened my mouth and words had emerged that I knew nothing about, spoken through my mouth, but by something other than myself.

I knew the words I'd just heard myself utter had spoken the truth. They were so powerful and clear. I knew my brother was going to be all right. I had no idea where those ideas had come from or who had used my voice to speak, so forcefully, through me, but I, at least, was greatly comforted by what I'd heard.

I traveled home periodically to be by his side through the various stages of his ordeal. He did have to endure chemotherapy, but fortunately one of the books we'd received as a gift from friends, *Love, Medicine & Miracles*, was by Dr. Bernie Siegel, then a surgeon at Yale.

In the book Dr. Siegel described visualization techniques that his patients and others were using to lessen the effects they experienced during chemotherapy. My brother read the book cover to cover, absorbed its contents, and imagined that the chemotherapy was honey as it entered his veins, soothing, healing, and making everything right.

He got through his rounds of chemo, only getting really sick the first day of the very first treatment. He went through two surgeries as well and has been fine through all of the decades since. My college graduation pictures show us beaming at the camera, my brother looking handsome and utterly bald.

When the voice speaks, whether to me or directly through me, it speaks the truth. I can misunderstand or misinterpret what I'm shown, often in highly symbolic images and impressions, but if I'm told something specific, it's true.

Walking the Plank

Before graduating from college I was living in a house with a number of other people, some students, some working full-time. The house had the camaraderie of big breakfasts eaten together once in a while on weekends or of meals cooked amid lots of laughter; it was a fun place to be, although located in a sketchy, dangerous, part of town.

I hadn't graduated yet because I still had my two incompletes to finish up; meanwhile I was working full-time at the lab, making pretty good money, and socking most of it away each month.

One of our roommates suddenly needed to move out to live closer to his work. I had gone to D.C. for a week-long training for my job, so I was out-of-town when my roommates conducted their initial interviews for a new roommate. Normally, this was a process that involved two or three steps as it was a big decision, but I returned home after a week away and found the roommates interviewing someone. I said hello, shook his hand, listened for two minutes, and then headed back out, rushing to not be too late to meet up with my friends. When I caught up with a couple of the roommates cooking in the kitchen the next day I said, "About that guy you were interviewing, I don't have a great feeling about him. I know I said I thought he'd be fine, but I'm having second thoughts. Something feels off."

"Oh, well, you said 'okay,' so we accepted him. He's already moved in." I had been on an all-night pub crawl, which was why I had dropped off my bag, thrown on some different clothes, and left right away the night before. Even though, for me, it had been a sober night of revelry, I'd had fun with a bunch of friends, ending with breakfast out. I'd come home and gone right to sleep. It was now later in the afternoon, and the guy had apparently moved his limited belongings in that very morning.

"What? We normally do a couple of interviews, take a little time to think things over. What happened?"

"Well, he seemed nice and he really needed a place to live right away, so we fast-tracked it."

"Oh. Well, I guess it'll be okay," I assured them, bracing myself to make the best of it. I hoped it wouldn't be like one of our other roommates with whom I'd already had a couple of uncomfortable conversations.

Him: "I thought we might date."

Me: "Well, I already have a boyfriend. You've met him. You know him."

Him: "But I thought that we might go out."

Me: "I'm not available. I'm already dating someone, as you know."

Him: "I thought that we could go out."

Me: "No. We can't." That guy wasn't evil; he just existed in a realm somewhere beyond the clueless. And he was studying to be a physician, his heart set on becoming a gynecologist. I found the thought pretty appalling. Other than him, though, whom I avoided as best I could, the roommates were a lot of fun. How bad could the new guy really be?

A little over a week later, I found out.

Fire in the Hold

I had some sort of stomach issue and had called in sick to work. Everyone else in the house was at work or at school. I was home sick in bed, although for some unaccountable reason, I was fully clothed. The only item of clothing I wasn't wearing was shoes.

When I had moved in it had been with the understanding that I would take the attic. I had plastered, sanded, and painted, and as a result, for an incredibly low monthly rent, I had the upstairs floor completely to myself. My roommates always knocked on the door and then called up the stairs before venturing up to my domain. I shared the bathroom one floor down with others, but other than that, I had three rooms (a sitting room, study, and bedroom in the far back) and a really large closet all to myself. It was spacious and really comfortable, although minimally furnished.

I was sleeping on top of the bed, which was a mattress on the floor, in jeans and a sweatshirt, when I heard the floorboards creak and woke up. I sat up on my bed as new weirdo roomie walked past me and sat down. He was a really tall guy, and he had just let himself into my space, come upstairs, walked through my study, entered my bedroom, and sat down on my bed. No one else was home.

He immediately placed his hand on my thigh. I started talking, in a really calm voice, about work or something, anything to distract him, and without looking at him. I carefully removed his hand, returning it to him. A little while later he put his hand back on my leg. I continued to talk about neutral topics and again removed his hand. I avoided all eye contact with him and forced myself to stay strangely calm, speaking in a slow, quiet, and neutral voice.

The process repeated itself again.

I knew I couldn't possibly outrun him. I'd have to stand up, get out of the bedroom, zip through the next room, down the set of stairs that led to the third floor, down two more flights of stairs, and then rush to the double front doors, one of which I would have to unlock with a key from the inside. I didn't stand a chance.

"Keep talking. Keep your voice low. Stay really calm and disinterested. Don't make eye contact." This information had appeared within me as a sort of knowing, not as a voice. Even the guidance I was receiving at the moment was trying to be really quiet and still.

The fourth time he put his hand on me, it felt different, harder, more determined. I didn't think I had much time left. Suddenly, without saying a word, he stood up and walked out of my room and went downstairs. I sat there as he walked out. It wasn't until he had gone down the stairs that I heard the barely audible sounds of the other female roommate, Anne, moving around in her room on the second floor. How he heard that from the fourth floor, I don't know, but he was clearly listening carefully for who else might be around.

I got up and walked down to Anne's room and knocked on the door. "What happened?" she immediately wanted to know. "You're pale as a ghost! What's wrong?" She invited me into her room, and I told her the story.

Meanwhile, scary dude had gone out.

When all the roommates had come home–he had come home too, but had gone straight up to his room–the rest of us talked about what had happened and about what to do. The police had come but had told us that since "we" had invited him to live with us, there was nothing, legally, that they could do. One of the officers, perhaps seeing the terrified look on my face, had turned toward me and quietly asked me, "Do you know anyone you could call?"

"Yes," it occurred to me, I did know someone persuasive whom I could call for help in getting this unwanted human out of the house, and permanently.

"I called my friend, a really kind, intellectual, big guy, and told him what had happened. Women were this roommate's prey, but he seemed furtive, afraid of being caught by someone who could really take him on. I was banking on him being afraid of my friend Joe, given Joe's size and forceful character. Joe was willing to give it a try.

A short while later Joe came over and went upstairs, opened the door to the guy's room, and didn't come out again until they both came out, a couple of hours later, the guy carrying his stuff.

"What happened," we were dying to know, after sicko freak had left. It was a pleasant fall evening, so we continued to hang out on the front porch, talking. "Well, I decided to do to him what he'd done to you, so I just walked into his room and sat down right near him. I didn't touch him, though, so that was different," he laughed to himself.

"Oh my God. What did he do? Weren't you scared?"

"No. He wasn't going to try anything with me. I

could immediately tell that he was intimidated by me. I'm a guy, and not a small guy, and he already knew the police had been here and that he was in trouble. He was scared, but he refused to leave."

"I think he's mentally ill," I said. "His appearance shifts sometimes. Did anyone else notice that? Sometimes he looks taller and sometimes shorter, earlier he seemed heavier, but the other day he looked almost thin, sometimes he seems almost normal, and sometimes he looks clearly psychotic. It's like those people with multiple personalities, and one personality has green eyes, one has brown eyes, one's allergic to cats, one plays the trombone, you know."

"Maybe," Joe answered, "but I really wasn't that interested in getting to know him or his problems. I just wanted him out. He told me that you had come on to him. I knew that wasn't true, but it was a way to get him talking, so I asked him how he'd met you. He told me he'd met you in a bar. Since I knew that that was impossible, I knew he was lying, that nothing else he would have to say would have merit, and that it was now just a waiting game."

"I'm staying," he insisted.

"I told him that that wasn't a problem, that this could take however long he liked, but that I wasn't going to leave his room until he did. No discussion. That that was how it was going to be."

The idiot had lasted about 90 minutes before he had started to pack up his things. A couple of days later he returned with the police to say that he had been unfairly treated and kicked out by his mean, crazy roommates.

We let him and the police into the house, everyone watching him warily. It so happened that we were enjoying a leisurely Sunday brunch at our long dining room table.

We must have looked like the most boring, uneventful, harmless group of 20-year-olds the police had seen in a while. They escorted him back out of our house, and he never returned.

Beyond, There be Monsters

Before the berserk house"mate" sat down on my bed, while I was working in the lab full-time and finishing up a couple of long-overdue papers, I was beginning to have visions of moving to Santa Fe, New Mexico. I could feel the place calling me, pulling me, trying to get me to move there. The problems, though, were several. I had a job, I needed to finish up the last bit of my degree, and I had never been to Santa Fe before and didn't know anyone who had lived or spent time there. I thought about moving west on a whim, talked about it a little with a couple of people, but I never mobilized myself and my resources to make the move. As I've learned, repeatedly, and very much the hard way, when Spirit guides you to do something, do it! Moving would have taken me away from what was about to happen next, which was the point, I think, of the guidance I was receiving to leave town.

The school year ended; I graduated, at long last, with a degree in just about everything, it seemed to me. I had taken so many more credits than I needed and in so many different fields that I was, then and now, a generalist who liked to look at an issue from a range of different perspectives. However, which field was I a master of, then or now? I'm still not quite sure.

Spring was drawing to a close, and I had just been fired from my job for objecting to my boss' continual, and, it should go without saying, utterly repulsive, sexual harassment. He was vulgar. He was rude. In short, a true pig.

Finally I'd had enough and told him to "fuck off" after he made a particularly disgusting remark, so he fired me. It was a huge relief, I thought to myself as I sat at the party that the office threw for me. Who gets fired and then gets a big party? Maybe someone who was grossly and unjustly treated every day she worked here? Definitely someone who had said out loud what everyone else who worked there had thought, and thought often. It was the 80's, yet even in the 90's there wasn't much one could do about harassment—just ask Anita Hill. Today, one wouldn't get away with it—at least I hope that that's true.

I had tried going over the head of the horrible manager, but my efforts at drawing attention to his inappropriate behavior and maybe even of getting it to stop, were received from the higher-ups with no interest, no support, and definitely no results.

My slate was suddenly clean. I was rid of the sticky stuff I'd step in every day when I showed up at the office, I'd graduated, and my apartment was one I could leave with very little notice to my roommates. I was free to move west, yet I still didn't. Instead, I made plans to take the cash I'd saved up and head to see friends in Europe then to start working in the Alps.

Climbing the Mast

One evening I remember sitting with a friend of mine, crying. "Why am I crying," I asked him. "I don't have any reason to cry," I insisted through tears I was completely unable to stop.

"My dad always told me that when we learn something important, we cry," he replied. I liked those words. They seemed sage and on point, but I had no idea what I was trying to learn.

I'd been feeling scared and on edge for a couple of days. I didn't know why I was scared, but I was. I had my friend wait outside until I got home and had locked the front door behind me. The next night, this time after spending time with Joe and a couple of other friends, they patiently waited in their car until I waved to them from the security of the living room. "I'm safe," I told myself. "I'm just being really careful. Everything's okay."

I went upstairs to my attic room to start packing for the trip I was taking in the morning to visit my grandparents in Florida. It wasn't Spring Break, but I'd often spent mine with G & G, as I called them (short for gram and gramps) at their little apartment, swimming in the pool of their building, going to the gay beach sometimes during the day (because I'd figured out that that was a beach that I could go to by myself and be blissfully left alone), reading novels on the balcony, catching up on family news, about which of their friends was sick or dying, about what I was going to do with my uncertain future, reviewing all the things I was not doing correctly in my life, including not having found a nice Jewish boy to marry, and going out for Early Bird dinners with them. It was going to be another full visit.

Other kids went on a crazy Spring Break or on vacation to drink and party; I went to visit G & G. Now I was going to see them before heading off to Europe for a while. The deal was, if I used my vacation to see them, they'd buy me the ticket. It was the perfect arrangement.

Meanwhile, I was in my room in the attic, and it was getting close to midnight as I finished packing my bag, my sense of dread continually growing.

"God," I spoke quietly into the room around me, "I feel like I'm about to die. Am I going to die?"

No response.

The sense of my impending death didn't dissipate, so I rephrased my question. "Is the plane I'm going to take tomorrow morning going to crash?"

"No, the plane is fine." Okay, well that was good news, for everyone planning to be on that plane in the morning, and for me too, if I lived that long. It was also good to discover that my guides were still speaking to me and that I could still hear them. Unfortunately, I didn't feel any better about my chances for living much longer. It felt like my time was almost up, and I hadn't even turned 25.

"Is something going to happen to the plane?" I've found that sometimes I need to phrase my question just right in order to get a useful answer.

"The plane is fine. Nothing is going to happen to the plane," came the clear and immediate reply.

"Then what is it? What's wrong? Why do I feel like I'm about to die?"

No response.

"Am I going to die? What's going on? What do I need to do?"

Complete and total radio silence. Not a word in reply.

"I can hear you just fine when you speak to me. We're having a conversation here. Why won't you tell me what's going on? I'm scared! Do I need to do something? What am I supposed to do?"

Again, the silence was deafening.

I zipped up my suitcase, arranged my purse, the book I was planning to read during the flight, and everything else I needed for the next day and got into bed. I was wearing a T-shirt and underwear. It was too hot to wear more, and the window of my fourth-story bedroom was cracked to let in a bit of air. I lay down on top of my bed, closed my eyes, and waited. I didn't know what I was waiting for, but there was no way I could fall asleep. It felt like I was on high alert.

Pirates on the Horizon

At 12:30am, exactly one half hour after I had turned off my light and lay down on the bed, I heard the teeniest, tiniest noise outside my window. Hearing noises in the old house where I lived was normal. That old wooden structure creaked and groaned with the best of them. Hearing noises outside of the house was normal as well. Cats complained and roamed, squirrels scurried, branches scraped the sides of the building–the little bits of noise in and around my room were an ordinary part of every day and every night. However, this time that littlest of noises felt like a siren.

"Open your eyes!" a voice screamed in my head.

I was terrified, my eyes shut tight as I gave my head a tiny shake.

"Open your eyes! Open your eyes right now!" the voice shrieked at me from within my head.

I opened my eyes and beheld a man climbing in through my window, four stories off the ground, with the agility of a monkey, the intentions of a madman.

All of this happened in the quickest of instants as I jumped up, ran out of my bedroom and through my "office," screaming my head off as I ran to the door that separated me from the stairs and which I had locked that night, although I had never locked it in the past because I lived safely with a group of other people.

"Calm down," I commanded myself, forcing my fumbling hands to focus on unlocking the door. The doorknob turned, and I began running down the stairs while screaming as loudly and continuously as is humanly possible. I ran down three flights of steps and reached the front door where I began to unlock it. I could hear someone pounding on the front door from the other side. Within moments of my starting to scream, Anne had started to scream as loudly as possible too. Both of us were still screaming our heads off.

I opened the front door to find the terrified next-door neighbor staring at me, "Are you okay," she gasped, her husband standing next to her. Was there some kind of weapon in his hand? I no longer remember what it was–a baseball bat, I think. "We heard people screaming bloody murder. We didn't know what was happening."

"I'm okay," I explained. "I think I'm okay," I reassured myself.

"Get off the damn phone," I yelled at the clueless roommate, turning around to curse he who had wanted to date me despite my opinion to the contrary, now yelling at him. He continued to talk on the phone that was attached to the kitchen wall, the only shared phone line we had coming into the house. As per usual, he was clueless, utterly clueless. Two of his roommates had been screaming their heads off, people were banging on the front door, trying to interrupt what sounded like a vicious murder, and he continued to talk to his mother. (I don't know for a fact that he was actually talking to his mother. She's just the only person I can think of he might have realistically been speaking with.) He was staring at me in my limited garb; I grabbed an apron and put it on.

"Hang up the goddamn phone. Hang it up. I have to

call the police, you f–ing idiot! If you don't hang up that phone…"

He hung up, holding the phone out to me as I dialed 911, his eyes wide and uncomprehending.

In the moments before the police got there, Anne and I had a chance to embrace. I filled her in as best I could with what had happened.

"I heard you screaming like you were dying, like you were being killed, so I started to scream too. It was the only thing I could think of to do. Just hearing you was terrifying!"

The police went with me up to my room.

"He escaped the same way he came in," they explained, showing me the path that he'd created for himself from a neighbor's house on the other side, up a ladder, across a ledge, to my windowsill.

"We know who this guy is. He's been raping women in the neighborhood at knifepoint. You're very, very lucky."

"If you f–ing know who he is, why hasn't he been arrested? Why isn't he in jail?" My manners on this particular night were non-existent.

"We recognize his pattern, his M.O. We don't actually have him yet, but we're looking for him."

"Why aren't there signs up all over the neighborhood warning us? Why aren't there posters everywhere so that we can be informed and extra-vigilant?" This is the sort of question that has been asked by many, many women at many, many prominent colleges and universities around the country. A rapist is on the loose in the area, but the college chooses to protect its image rather than its students and employees. Disgusting. An appalling and an appallingly common stance. And dangerous. That night it was very dangerous for me. That had been a close call, a really, really close call.

Buoys

After I'd had some time to calm down, after people had stopped sleeping on my bedroom floor to help me feel safe, an endless slumber party, I began to ask my guides to explain themselves.

"Why? Why in the world did you let that happen? I was almost viciously raped! I was almost murdered! How could you let that happen?"

It had come to me, clearly, that had the intruder managed to take the three steps to my bed and put his knife to my neck, I would have died. I would have struggled and I would have died a violent, degrading, humiliating, painful, and terrifying death.

"Why? I was listening to you! I was talking to you! I was trying to do what you told me! Why couldn't you have warned me? Why couldn't you have gotten me out of the house, away from there, spared me that entire, horrifying ordeal? Why?"

I was absolutely furious. Yes, I had survived, with perhaps a couple of seconds to spare. The only thing I was grateful for was that I never saw the bastard's face. He was climbing in the window and had one leg and his butt through the window and was pulling the rest of his body into my room when I had started to scream and run. It was horrifying. No one should ever have to go through such an experience–not any part of it.

Little by little, I was a bit less traumatized, but I didn't manage to fully clear the horror and trauma of that day for years, until I learned and practiced the tapping technique, EFT, on myself for this and related issues. If you've got pain, a phobia, traumas of any kind in your past–it doesn't really matter what the difficult situation and events were–take a moment to look up and study some EFT techniques. Then learn how to use them to release pain, anxiety, and trauma; it's surprisingly easy. Then use those tapping techniques, over and over again, releasing the past as you go. It's simple, it's free, and it's incredibly effective.

Soon after that scary night, I left for Europe, but I was badly shaken. It was hard to trust my guides and the guidance I was and wasn't getting, and it was difficult to see the world as a safe and decent place. The world often isn't a safe place, and very often some of the people in it are not decent, perhaps not decent at all. I knew that and had experienced other kinds of misery at the hands of my fellow humans, but it was still a painful reminder of the hardship and suffering in the world, of how fragile we all are, of the darkness and storms and sea monsters that lurked in the dangerous depths.

Aye, Aye, Captain

"Why?" I continued to plague the angels who had been so loving and helpful to me in the past, who through me had even been helpful to other people (and surely them to me as well, but I can't recount other people's guidance and promptings from the angelic realm, just my own).

"Why?"

I don't know that I've ever had an answer that has completely satisfied me, but I've received answers, and they're not too different from the ones I got when hitchhiking across Europe a few months later.

"If you'll remember, we tried to get you to move away from the city and to go to Santa Fe where you would have been safe from these events, but you didn't want to go. That's okay. You are free to decide to do whatever you want, to listen to us or not, to make your own choices or to follow our recommendations. That's up to you. Of course, all choices have consequences. We're not punishing you for not having listened, but that decision led to a life-threatening situation."

"We're teaching you to listen and respond without question. We're teaching you to trust us and to stop trying to lead your life yourself. Let us lead. Ask us to take over everything. The more we take over your life, the better it will be."

"I'm trying to do that," I insisted. "I really am." And I was, but it would still be a number of years before I finally and fully let go of the rudder of my life, before I truly "Let go, and let God." I still had too many opinions about what I wanted, about what was right or wrong for me, about what my life should look like and how it should unfold. There was still a lot of "me" in myself, and it was trying to run my life.

"If, one day, you learn to utterly rely on and trust us, we could lead you through a minefield unscathed. We could take you anywhere, under any circumstances, and no harm could befall you. If you can place yourself in our hands without reservations, then you will be safe and all will be well."

"Nothing bad will ever happen to me again?"

"Of course hard things will still happen, people will still get sick, people will still die, you will still experience pain and loss and a whole range of experiences that you would probably call 'bad,' although still necessary."

"I don't understand how you're helping me be safe and well, then. True, it's exciting to talk to you, at least most of the time. You've been really helpful to me a bunch of times. Through me you've given helpful information to my friends, even when they thought it was really weird. Anne was frantic the other night when she couldn't find her wallet after two days of searching, and then I walked into the chaos of her room and said, pointing, 'It's in the pocket of those pants there,' listening to the words as they escaped my mouth. There are so many times you've given useful guidance that made things easier, simpler, wiser. Thank you, but I don't know why you can't make my life better still."

"We can, and we will, to the extent you allow. Stop thinking you know. Stop trying to control things. Stop thinking of yourself and about yourself and for yourself so much. That's ego, not the truth of your being."

"Why am I here then?"

"You have this life because you chose it, including where you'd be born and to whom. You knew there would be hardships, even though the details for the most part weren't known to you in advance. You accepted that you would go through life often having no idea what was coming next–just like everyone else. You need to have those experiences so that you can remember what it feels like to be a typical person who doesn't have glimpses into the future, who doesn't receive warnings of difficult times or hear a comforting voice from beyond when things get really tough."

"You need to understand what most other people go through and how they feel. You need to experience some of the same hardships, the same kinds of problems, the same fears and pain and losses. If not, how will you be able to help them heal, help guide them to a healthier and deeper way of living in the world? How will they be able to trust you unless you're able, not just to hear and talk about the wisdom you receive from the higher realms, but also of the very ordinary pain and human suffering that weaves its way through the lives of most people. You can't be too different. You have plenty of lessons to learn too. You have karma to repay. You need certain kinds of experiences to develop empathy and insight and in order to grow. You can't be too safe."

"You need to live a full life, an authentic life, a life that has known hardship and sorrow as well as ease and joy. By working through the pain you will become more honest, more authentic, more helpful. By making your way through the tough times, by learning from the lessons those dark experiences contain, you will begin to heal, you will become wiser, healthier, more whole. You will become the person, the writer, the teacher, and the guide that we need you to be."

What can a person say to that? It is an honor to be trusted with so great a task. It's a double-edge sword, the knowing about terrible things that are on their way while having no ability to stop them. Sometimes I think it would be better not to know in advance about what's coming, and sometimes I don't have a clue as to what's on the horizon. Knowing is hard. Not knowing, perhaps, is harder. More common, more typical, but more difficult in the end, I think.

I need to learn acceptance, I reflected to myself. I need to deepen in my faith that there is a plan for me and for us all, and that this plan, at its core, is good. I need to practice gratitude.

Truly, giving thanks is the highest form of prayer, one that I need to continue to lean into more each day.

The Compass

Somehow, it took the death of my first husband, the one I was yet to meet, for me to finally reconcile myself to the voices and messages that were trying to lead and guide me. Until then, I'd argued with them constantly. I'd questioned them and demonstrated a great reluctance to follow and to believe, truly, in them and in what they were trying to do for me. Before then, I hadn't wanted to accept my abilities, these strange gifts that seemed so impossible. I couldn't talk to most people about these voices and visions; much of the time I didn't really understand what they were communicating to me, or why, and they made me feel so different from most of the people I knew, or even knew about, that I often felt I was on an uncharted voyage with nothing to guide me.

Yes, I'd become more spiritual over the years; I'd started to read spiritual books and I prayed more and more often, but I wanted guidance, information, teachings, as I now consider them, to show up where, when, and how I wanted. I wanted to be in charge, in control, even of the guidance received. I wanted my life and the help I was receiving to show up on my terms.

Overcoming this "wanting it my way" is one of the biggest lessons I've had to learn, and I believe that it is one of the most important lessons anyone can accept. To whom does your life belong? Who is its creator? Who is truly in charge? Do you really think it should be you? I finally figured out that it definitely shouldn't be me!

I hadn't yet learned to simply accept, trust, and follow. I hadn't yet learned to embrace these gifts and say thank you with all my heart, no matter what I was or wasn't told. I was still trying to live my life my way.

Now I realize how much I need these helpers and their wisdom. Now I am afraid to try to do things on my own, but the illusion of having control over myself and in my life was hard to give up completely.

As I began in my thirties to acknowledge that these voices really were on my side, that they were trying to prepare me and help me through life, and that they knew what they were talking about, I wanted more. Once I'd figured out that these beings were genuinely benevolent and could help me, I wanted them to continue. "What's going to happen next? What should I do with my life? What kind of work should I pursue? Does my shirt match these pants?" It's like having your own personal oracle, only it turns out that it doesn't work that way, at least not for me.

The trumpeting voice, the one that spoke with such force and vision piped in from some other realm, has only spoken to me once in a while before and since that loud wedding day, and always in a single sentence or two, and then only if there were something specific that I needed to know or do. When I hear the loudspeaker voice, I know I need to pay careful attention, that I need to act, that my life is changing course, or that I'm being prepared to do something. Usually, my own free will to be a complete idiot is fully respected by the guides in the higher echelons, but once in a while they seem to have permission to grab the megaphone and blare like a fog horn through the mists with which I'm surrounded in order to help me, if I really listen and follow carefully, to steer clear of the rocks, to avoid hidden sand bars, and to escape treacherous waters.

Yes, I'd received guidance since I was a small child, but mostly the voice could best be described as "small." I'd also had experiences of simply knowing something external to my personal experience whether "speaking" through me or to me through feelings, thoughts, images, impressions, or bodily sensations, guiding me in one direction or another. However, not only did I not discuss these events with others, I didn't think about them very often myself. I took in the information without really reflecting on it too much. I usually did what I felt prompted to do, but my response didn't feel like a following so much as that of a trusting child leaning on Grandma's side as she reads a story. Now, though, I was an adult, and adults need to make adult decisions. As an adult, I had much more freedom in my daily life, I had bigger decisions to make, and I felt like I was being held increasingly accountable for my choices; the bar was being raised–more was being expected of me.

I began to be aware of a second voice, subtle and interior, difficult to distinguish from my ordinary thoughts except that it possessed a deeper stillness and clarity than my own mode of self-expression. This voice began to offer comment with greater frequency, and after a while I would have conversations with myself: regular me and smarter me.

Regular Me: "Where in the world am I going to park?" I say to myself, not expecting a response.

Smarter Me, a.k.a., Inner Font of Wisdom: "Turn left," I suddenly hear a response, realizing that I'm not alone in my thoughts.

Me, going with it: "Left? There won't be anything to the left. That way is always full."

Inner Font: "Turn left."

Me: "Okay, fine. Wait. I don't believe it! What total luck."

Inner Font: "It wasn't luck."

Ordinary stuff for the most part, but helpful. Unfortunately, I often chose not to listen to those inner proddings. Learning to listen comprised an almost flat and seemingly endless learning curve. This curve didn't even constitute a gentle slope. A learning .01% grade was more like it. We continued this generally fruitless conversation for years.

Inner Font of Wisdom: "If you park in front of that house you will get a nail in your tire."

Moi: "That's ridiculous. Why would there be a nail there?"

Inner Font, Silent, not saying a word, but probably thinking: "You're going to regret this. Why do you insist on making things difficult for yourself?"

I park my car where I want, get out, and walk a little ways, which is when I realize that there's a teenager standing nearby, previously hidden from view, holding a bunch of nails in his hand, nails that he was using to tinker with a teenage sort of project. I look back at my car. Is it just me, or is it somewhat lopsided? I move in closer for inspection. My left front tire is slowly deflating before me, and, naturally, in front of the teenage boy who has come over to see what's of such interest, now no longer holding a bunch of nails in his hand. Rule One of Teenagedom: hide the evidence.

Now, I would think that any sane, regular person would, after two or three times of not following what was clearly good, if often illogical, advice, begin to carefully follow every whisper, even if it didn't make any sense and even if it conflicted with one's previous plans. Instead I ignored the wisdom of this inner voice over and over again, insisting that I myself knew what was best for me. Apparently not.

Is my astrological chart full of Taurus, the utterly stubborn? Mercury going retrograde (whatever that means) is apparently a bad thing. Is Mercury on a permanent backward spin in my chart? Or was it just me, so scared of thinking new, different, and bigger sorts of thoughts, clinging frantically to the sinking life raft of my old world view when there was a cruise ship teeming with amenities lolling happily nearby, just waiting to throw me a life line if only I would stop refusing to grab it? I began to suspect that this cruise ship might be where the lunch lady lived. My brown bag lunch with a dented peanut butter and jelly sandwich, soggy in the middle, was familiar and safe, and it remained stuck to the roof of my mouth long after I should have developed a more sophisticated palate.

Sand in My Suit

I struggled with my ever-developing psychic abilities. Basically, I hated them. They were weird, unwanted, and made me feel completely out-of-control. And they kept getting worse. By worse I mean more frequent. And stronger. What many people would term "better."

I would console myself with the thought, "Well, even if I hear voices, at least I don't have visions." I would feel relieved for a few months until the visions started occurring. I would then wrestle internally with this new development, feel like I was going crazy for a while, notice that this new ability was really helpful to me and to others, begin to make some peace with it, and then a new thought would occur to me. "Well, at least I don't know what other people are thinking. That would really be awful–I can barely stand to listen to my own thoughts."

Next thing I knew, snippets of the conversations rattling around in the heads of passersby would begin to impinge on my consciousness. I fought that one pretty hard and eventually made some sort of deal with whatever is in charge that I was only willing to hear the goings on in another's mind if it were really important for me to know, such as if that peculiar ambulatory personality was particularly perverse and looking to intrude on the sanctity of my being. In other words, if he were potentially dangerous. Then I wanted to know enough of what was going on in his twisted thoughts to be guided to take the appropriate evasive action such as, "Turn left."

The eavesdropping fortunately calmed down and, since I had apparently learned nothing from all that came before, I would let my mind wander and suddenly think, "Well, at least I've never experienced remote viewing."

Once a new mode of perception began, it never left, although that didn't mean that I could control it or that it would happen often. It was now just another surprise added to my involuntary repertoire that would spring out at me when least expected. I saw myself as some sort of modern Pandora walking down the street carrying a jack-in-the-box, unable to put it down and half-hoping, half-dreading that it would spring open at any moment.

I think that Pandora, whose name means "all gifts" in Greek, has been misunderstood and misrepresented by history. I can't really blame those around her for not getting it; these "gifts" weren't happening to someone else, they were happening to me and I didn't get it either.

If the mythical box Pandora opened really contained all gifts, would it have brought forth misery, pain, suffering, fear, and other sorts of awfulness with the one small positive gift of hope as the only salve? "All gifts" means *all*. A great loss, such as a divorce or an illness, can bring about deep personal growth, insight, and forward momentum on one's life path, so in that sense an illness, given time and the proper perspective, could be looked at as a sort of disguised gift. I'd often seen it happen. Some gifts, masquerading as misery or misfortune, would eventually bring about deep lessons, greater compassion, wisdom, or other kinds of rewards.

Yet I'm sure that Pandora's box also contained all

the gifts that look beautiful at first glance as well, not just lonely hope. Surely she had joy in there, and love, and peace, humor, wit, good hair days, and raucous laughter in the company of friends. My personal Pandora, at least, seemed to want to make my life easier and happier, guiding me to tasty condiments and warming soups whenever I would allow it, to the healthier choices in that lunch counter line. Why wouldn't I let her just take over?

Desert Island

The year I finally graduated from college, I lived in Berlin for a time. Having more and more visions in high school and during college was emotionally unsettling, to say the very least. Eventually those experiences led to a sound and stable emotional equilibrium, but for a number of years the increasing frequency and variety of my "psychic" experiences was disturbing, frightening at times, exhilarating, and very confusing. It definitely did not help me focus on my studies or graduate quickly from the college where I was enrolled, a very left-brained and rationalistic kind of place, at least at that time, and at least in my personal experience.

I ended up living in Berlin, but my carefully laid plans were for me to live in France. I don't know what the status of things are now in France and in Europe in general, especially after the establishment of the Eurozone, but at that time it was possible to pay a small sum to receive a visa to work in France for three months as long as one started to work during the same calendar year in which one graduated from college. I got an International Student ID card, I got an International Youth Hostel card, and I arranged for a work visa for France. I was all set. First I was going to visit friends elsewhere in Europe, and then I was going to travel to France to find a job. It was my plan to get a job, cleaning toilets, washing dishes, whatever, in a ski resort in the Alps in France. That sounded good to me. I figured that I could spend time in Europe while working on my French and my skiing in a beautiful setting all at the same time. I had a plan, and it was a good one. Maybe one of my best!

While traveling in Europe a friend from the States joined me for a few days in Greece. I'd been to Greece before, so I assumed the role of tour guide, making sure that we visited the Acropolis, Plaka in the old part of Athens, Poseidon's Temple at Sounion, and, of course, the island of Santorini. You've seen the pictures–white buildings perched on the rim of a volcano that overlook a profoundly blue sea very far below. A bit treacherous perhaps, but gorgeous!

While on the island I was offered a job working at the youth hostel there. That youth hostel card I'd lined up was already coming in handy. First I got a cheap place to stay, and then I got a job at the same place. I said "bon voyage" to my friend who was about to begin a month-long train trip through Europe from east to west, and I started work in the youth hostel. The pay included a bunk bed in the girls' dorm, some food, and not quite enough pay to survive from month to month. Not the best job I've ever had by any stretch of the imagination, but it was fun.

It was my job to cook breakfast every morning for the guests. The choices on the menu were eggs. They could be served scrambled, fried, hard or soft boiled, or in a sort of omelet (in the hands of another "chef" actual omelets would have been possible), and that was it. There was no poaching of eggs done by me. I suppose there was also bread and jam, but since I didn't have to cook them, they don't linger in my mind. Was there also yogurt on offer? Probably. Juice? Same issue.

The kitchen could be described as rustic and minimalistic by someone with a highly active imagination and a surprisingly optimistic and rosy view of the world and all it contained. At my disposal were spices in four unlabeled jars. I quickly identified the salt and pepper. It didn't take me long to figure out that the third jar contained oregano. This was Greece, after all. I figured out what was in the fourth jar when a very polite young German man walked up to the counter holding his "omelet" with a rather astonished look on his face, tentatively asking me, "Could I please have another one without cinnamon?"

"Of course," I replied, grateful to now know what was in jar number four. A part of me wondered why I had been allowed to happily cook, albeit rather poorly, eggs for any number of young travelers, all of them with a light sprinkling of cinnamon on them. I suppose that those adventuresome voyagers returned to their various home ports to tell their friends and family that the Greeks put cinnamon on their eggs. Just to set the record straight, they don't. They really don't. That was just me being something of an idiot. Thank you, brave and anonymous German traveler with the excellent manners.

Palm Trees and Coconuts

This period of my life occupies a rather flimsy area of my mind, so I can't tell you exactly how long I worked in the youth hostel, but I did eventually graduate from the large dorm to one of the little rooms on the roof. Think of the smallest, most basic, haphazardly and only partially white-washed, mattress on the floor, unfettered by any sort of modern convenience beyond the one light bulb dangling from the ceiling, cell imaginable, then make it a lot smaller and less attractive. That was my room, and I considered it a raise.

Those of us who worked in the youth hostel, beyond the owners, that is (who collected the money–that was their job), were allowed to cook food for ourselves in the kitchen. We were allowed to cook whatever we had purchased along with items found in their limited pantry. The limited pantry, if memory serves, contained burger patties in the freezer. With the addition of the purchase of a large bag of rice, and some tomatoes, onions, and green peppers in town, I was able to prepare meals. In the evenings I would often cook dinner for myself and a woman from Australia. She had the unenviable job of emptying the "dunny bins," as she called them, and of cleaning the toilets and showers. She did it with an unfailingly good sense of humor. For those of you who might travel to an island or some other similar destination one day, the dunny bins, placed next to toilets in locales with sketchy plumbing, are little trash cans with plastic bags in them into which one throws used toilet paper because the toilets there can probably handle human waste and some water, but nothing else.

For our dinners I made ground beef on rice, ground beef in rice, rice on ground beef and, on one triumphant occasion, peppers and tomatoes stuffed with ground beef and rice. The other people who worked at the hostel turned out for that meal, which surprised me more than anyone since I hadn't realized that I knew how to make Greek stuffed peppers and tomatoes.

Janice, the bubbly Australian, was a lot of fun and greeted me every morning with a rousing, "Good morning, idiot," "Good morning, dick head," and other similar salutations. I was unable to argue with any of them, and we became friends.

When the tourist season came to a final end in late fall, the last of the intrepid travelers willing to admit that Greek islands really are cold and damp and windy in the winter, the youth hostel closed, and I headed back to Athens to purchase a bus ticket to France. The "Magic Bus," as it was called, was cheap and drove day and night, with occasional stops for bathroom breaks, from Athens to Paris, and perhaps to points beyond, making various stops on its route. This land route was designed before the dismantling of the former Soviet Union and Soviet Bloc, so we traveled through what was then Yugoslavia before weaving around mountains in Switzerland and continuing on to France. I enjoyed the views as I ate meatballs and hard-boiled eggs and read novels I'd traded with other travelers for books I'd finished. From Paris I got the train to Annecy, a lovely town near the base of the French Alps.

Beginning in Athens, even before I bought my bus ticket to France, I began to hear a voice. It wasn't particularly welcome, and it really didn't make much sense to me at all, but it said to me, periodically, over and over again, "Go to Berlin." Of course, I understood what the words "Go to Berlin" meant, but I was heading to France. I didn't have any plans to go to Berlin or even to visit Germany. All my arrangements were for France.

I ignored the voice as I bought my bus ticket. I ignored the voice as I traveled across Europe, to Paris, and then on to Annecy. It was raining and late afternoon when I arrived in Annecy, and I was on a budget, so I hiked down roads and all the long way up the hill on which the local youth hostel was perched. I spent the next couple of days wandering around Annecy, ignoring the voice telling me to head to Berlin and talking to people about jobs at ski resorts, jobs which everyone I spoke to assured me didn't exist at the moment. I met lots of other people who had come to this part of France from various places for similar reasons.

"The ski resorts aren't hiring yet. There isn't any snow so far this season. It looks like it's not going to be a very good year for the resorts. Maybe they'll start getting snow in December or January, but they aren't hiring yet."

"Go to Berlin," the voice in my head clamored, more and more insistently.

Full Speed Ahead

On my third morning there, a Sunday, I awoke to find that the woman who had been in another dorm room two days before, and who had last night moved into my dorm, was now lying in the bed right across from me, looking at me expectantly. She had seemed quite lost and more than a little interested in me as I politely never expressed any interest in return. She wasn't getting the hint, and she was not getting it in closer and closer proximity to me. Unwanted amorous attention was one of the hazards of independent travel and was the chief reason why, since leaving Greece and its beach season, I let my leg hair grow, unfettered, into a rather long and curly mass. I'd used the leg hair ploy before to great effect–it deterred almost everyone. Of course, I was in France now, so perhaps this strategy was of limited usefulness.

"Go to Berlin now!" By now, the voice was practically yelling in my head. I hadn't been completely ignoring the voice. I'd been explaining to the voice that I wasn't going to Berlin; I was going to France to get a job as planned.

"Go to Berlin!" was pretty much all it ever said, but this morning it had added an emphatic "Now!" to its phrasing. I was getting a bit better at listening to the guidance I received, but this time I had a plan in place that I really liked and was committed to. Besides, I only knew one person in Berlin, a guy I'd started to date a little bit on the island. We'd exchanged addresses, sure, but it had seemed likely that we wouldn't be seeing each other again.

"Go to Berlin now!"

"It's Sunday," I replied, "and I don't have much money, and what I have is in dollars and French francs. The banks aren't open on Sunday, so I don't have a way to get any more. I can't buy a train ticket without money. I don't have a way to get to Berlin today."

"Go to Berlin now!"

At this point, if you're old enough, as I am, to remember a time before the Internet, before ATM machines and bank cards, and to recall travelers checks, you'll know that what I'm saying is true. There wasn't a way to get currency unless you went to a bank or an exchange center to cash travelers checks into the local currency. Perhaps in large airports it was different, but in cities, including in small ones like Annecy, the banks were firmly closed on Sundays.

"Go to Berlin now!"

"The only way I can go to Berlin now," I told the voice, at wit's end, "would be if I hitchhiked!"

"Okay."

"What?" This was the first new thing the voice had said to me in almost two weeks, and what it had to say was that I should hitchhike? Alone? Female and alone?

"Are you kidding? That's dangerous! I've never hitchhiked before. I promised myself I'd never hitchhike."

"We will be with you. You will be fine. Go to Berlin now!"

"To get to Berlin I have to cross borders!" (and by "Berlin," I meant, and the voice meant, "West Berlin"), "I'll have to go through East Germany!"

"It'll be fine. Everything will be fine."

Oh my God, I thought. I can't believe this. Not only am I being told to go to Berlin, hitchhiking with very little money, by myself as a young woman, I'm going to have to figure out how to cross national borders and get through East Germany, a devoted member of the Soviet Bloc, and then into West Berlin, a walled city with armed men posted in towers, a city I'd never been to before. Really, this was pushing the limit, even for me.

"Go to Berlin now!" The urgency was unmistakable. This wasn't a suggestion; this was an order. It probably had always been an order, right from the first time I'd heard it, but I'd finally figured out that the voice was not going to accept "no" as an answer and that, for whatever reason, I needed to get to Berlin and I needed to leave immediately.

I walked down to the communal kitchen to make myself some breakfast from the little stash of food I had with me. Bread, I assume, and some sausage. Other youth hostellers mingled there eating as well.

"I'm thinking of hitchhiking to Berlin," I told the couple finishing their cereal at the table where I was sitting.

"Really? Well if you can be ready in 10 minutes, we'll give you a ride to the entrance of the highway."

Suddenly the situation was urgent as I remembered my long, rainy, and exhausting hike up to the Youth Hostel. The thought of trudging the miles to the highway entrance (which I'd have to figure out how to get to) with my pack on my back was really unpleasant. And yes, it was raining steadily at this point and looked like it planned to continue doing so all day. Clearly, not only were my personal plans not of great interest to my guides, my personal comfort was not a priority for them either.

"I'll get ready right away! Thanks!" I jumped up and ran to my dorm to stuff my belongings back into my pack.

The Lee Shore: Protected from

the Wind

The couple, from Ireland, I think, dropped me just before the entrance to the highway and headed on their way. The rain had stopped, so I wasn't uncomfortable as I stood there and stuck out my thumb. After watching me for a couple of minutes, utterly befuddled, the man at the service station across the street called out to me.

"Where are you going?"

"Berlin," I replied. He shook his head in disbelief and then waved me over. "You'll need a sign," he said as he walked to the back of the service area, returning a few moments later with the side cut from a cardboard box and a large black marker. "You have to have a sign or you'll never get there." Clearly, I was a complete amateur at hitchhiking, which was more than I ever thought I'd be in regards to hitchhiking, something I had been sure I would never, ever do. Talk about being asked to trust. A 25-year-old buxom, single hitchhiker? This was about as bad an idea as any I'd heard of, and I was the one doing it.

I made my sign, thanked the guy, and headed back across the road. Within a couple of minutes a man heading north picked me up. We began to chat a bit in French. He was a local and he apologized when, after a while, he told me that he was so sorry, but he was going to have to let me out again in a few miles. Why was he sorry? Because within a couple of minutes of getting into his car it had begun to rain, and I mean really, really rain. A complete downpour was underway on the other side of my passenger window.

"I'll let you off before I exit," he said. "Are you really going all the way to Berlin?"

"Yes, that's my plan."

"How are you going to cross the borders?" He wanted to know.

"I don't really know. I guess I'll walk across."

"Good luck. I hope you have a safe trip." The man was a complete gentleman. I'm hitchhiking in Europe, I reminded myself. That's probably much less dangerous than hitchhiking in the States.

I thanked him and got out of the car, looking at my surroundings and at the grass by the side of the road, glistening with drops of rains from the deluge that had stopped just a couple of minutes before. This isn't so bad, I thought, as I held up my sign again and stuck out my thumb. I didn't wait three minutes before another car stopped to pick me up. This is true. I promise you this is true: It immediately began to rain again. It was cats and dogs territory. The rain began to pour down just as we drove off.

This time I was picked up by a car with three young people in it, probably experienced hitchhikers themselves. They were in high spirits as we talked a bit and they told me how crazy they thought it was that I was trying to hitchhike all the way to Berlin. For context, for those Americans reading this who are really bad at geography, which, being Americans might be many of them, this was a bit like putting out a sign and a thumb in Greeley, Colorado (it's a smallish town near Denver) that said "Anchorage" on it. Borders would need to be crossed–twice. Lots of mountains and territory would be in the way. The difference here is that the distances were somewhat shorter and the borders definitely more difficult. Also, there was that whole issue of East Germany, of machine guns, and the Cold War.

"What I'm going to do, the driver explained to me, is I'm going to let you out right before the Swiss border coming up." He didn't bother to apologize about letting me out in a deluge because the rain had just stopped once again. "I'm sorry, but I don't know you. You understand. I just can't risk having you in my car when we cross the border. You can cross on foot and then start hitchhiking again on the other side." He seemed a bit sheepish, and he had the thought "she's a potential drug runner–can't risk it–why else would she be hitchhiking across international frontiers" written all over his face as he looked at me.

"Of course. I completely understand. That's a great idea. Thank you so much."

I got out of the car, we waved, and I headed toward the house-like station which constituted the Swiss border crossing. The chalet-style building might have looked a bit casual, but this was the Swiss we're talking about. They're not a casual people, on the whole.

We were in the mountains now, the air was thinner and fresh, and the various guards, guns slung over their shoulders, were studying me as I approached. I gathered, from their stares and the ensuing conversation, that a lone woman crossing their border on foot was just not something they'd often encountered. I assume it had happened before. Probably, right? I can't have been the only fool to have ever tried that stunt?

I was led into the main office, asked a few questions and asked, of course, to review the contents of my pack. In the end they were very pleasant, charming even, as they chuckled at me and sent me on my way. They suggested I walk on a bit further before resuming my hitchhiking.

Once I'd made my way down the road a ways I stuck my thumb out again and was immediately picked up. So far, the trip had been surprisingly easy. And dry.

Sharks in the Water

"You're lucky you haven't gotten wet hitchhiking today," he told me. "It's supposed to rain hard all day."

My new driver and I had a pleasant visit as we watched the rain resume falling with a vengeance. Inevitably, of course, after a while, he told me how sorry he was, and how he regretted it, but his exit was coming up shortly and he needed to let me out in a few miles. There was nothing he could do about it, but he was awfully sorry I was about to get so drenched.

"Not a problem," I assured him as I thanked him for picking me up and helping me further on my way. By the time I stepped out of his car the clouds had decided to just be clouds for a bit, floating along without releasing any moisture at all, and once again I remained dry as I waited for my next ride, the only unnerving one of the journey.

The truck driver was from Turkey, he explained to me as he ogled me, speaking to me in German, his fairly adequate and mine truly terrible. I decided, on the spot, that for this leg of the journey I was Greek, a culture similar to its cousins across the Aegean Sea where they spoke a language he was unlikely to know at all. No, I was not an American, with their reputation for women with a spirit of adventure, a concept promoted by movies in which young people meet and fall into bed together a few frames later. Even though he was Turkish, I needed to be Greek. He leered at me and studied me, and I stayed firm in my Greek identity, throwing some tourist Greek at him for good measure. My manner was cold, and I stuck to the story that I had decided upon, expressed in lousy German, that I was headed to Berlin to get married. My future husband was waiting for me there. Listening to myself, my tale sounded silly and absurdly implausible, but I delivered it with all of the sincerity and belief that I could bring to my limited German vocabulary and more limited German grammar. The tale was true. I believed in it. I was a Greek (the virgin bit was implied, not stated) from a poor family heading to a new opportunity and life in Germany.

The rain had begun again, but I just couldn't worry about it, partly because by now I'd learned that it would stop whenever I needed to get out of a vehicle and partly because my right hand was gripped around my open Swiss Army Knife, just out of sight, and I was ready to do whatever was necessary to fulfill my promise of getting to Berlin.

It was with a great sense relief that I exited his truck at the rest stop where he deposited me. We went our separate ways as I gave thanks to the skies, once again clear, and to the promise I'd been given by my guiding angels that they would take care of me and keep me safe. Apparently that promise even extended to the weather. Apparently, though, they couldn't eliminate all creepy guys from the face of the planet or even from my path, although they could constrain their behavior.

The rest stop was welcome, and I remember getting a little something to eat although I'm no longer sure how I paid for my meal. Probably, I'd had the chance to convert a little money into Swiss francs while going through Switzerland on the Magic Bus the week before. After walking around the rest stop for a bit, I headed out into the parking lot to seek another ride.

Hidden Cove

A young man in a fast, sporty car picked me up right away as the light faded in the sky. "I'm going to Zurich," he told me. He was studying business there. He had an American woman as a roommate. She was studying dentistry, I think he told me, although I never understood how she came to decide that Zurich was where she needed to pursue her studies. "You'll like her. You'll have a lot in common. You'll stay with us tonight. We have an extra room in the apartment."

"That's so kind," I told him, "but I'll just stay at the train station in town." Every European city of any size at all has a train station, and Zurich was a major, cosmopolitan center, so it was a safe bet. "Just drop me off there. That'll be fine." We were speaking English, not German, which was a relief and much more successful. He was clearly well-educated, and as an MBA student his English needed to be good and it was.

"No, no, I insist. It's no trouble. I'll give you the spare key. You can visit Zurich, even stay a few days. It's a great city."

"The train station will be perfect," I assured him. "It will be fine to spend the night there. I'm in a bit of a hurry to get to Berlin." We talked about other things returning to this topic once in a while. Finally I understood that part of my guides' package deal for getting me to Berlin was a safe and comfortable place to spend the night, for free. In the end, I accepted.

"Great," he enthused. "You can make dinner for us in exchange," he explained as we made a quick stop at a grocery store for provisions. I gathered that neither he nor his roommate could cook, and perhaps they thought, optimistically, that I could. We had a very pleasant conversation over the disappointing meal that I prepared for them, but they were both too polite to comment on my cooking skills. I took some comfort in the thought that, rather pathetic though the meal was, maybe it was better than what they usually attempted for themselves.

I was given a key to their apartment and spent the next day touring the city, which was fun, and my guiding angels didn't bother me at all about hurrying on to Berlin. However, the following morning they started in again, as soon as I woke up, with their usual insistent statement, "Go to Berlin now."

At breakfast the two students were surprised at my claim that I needed to continue on my journey right away.

"Why not stay for a couple of days and see the sights? There's lots to do here and you have a key and can make yourself at home."

"Thank you so much, but I really need to get to Berlin quickly. I'm expected."

"But it's raining so hard out. It's supposed to rain and thunder all day. The trip will be miserable."

"Really, it's okay. I'll be fine. I don't mind the weather. I just need to try to get to Berlin today, if possible."

"Okay. I'll drop you off at the entrance to the

highway on my way to the university, but you don't need to do this."

I couldn't explain to them that I actually didn't think I'd be getting wet at all today. I couldn't tell them about the profound insistence in the voice that kept urging me onward. I could only thank them for their kindness and hospitality and continue my journey to Berlin.

As per usual, I was picked up right away by another car and didn't get wet at all that day either despite the lousy weather so typical for northern and central Europe at this time of year.

Treasure Island

The day I left Zurich would be tricky, though, because I would have to enter East Germany and, from there, travel into West Berlin, the guarded and isolated city then marooned in the midst of the Soviet Bloc.

A couple of rides later I was given a ride by a German man with a nice car who explained to me that he lived in Berlin. He wanted to know why I was headed there, and I explained that I had some friends here, which was something of an exaggeration, but I decided that while hitchhiking, telling the full truth might not be necessary. I had started to call the guy I knew who was a student in Berlin while I was in Annecy, France, in an attempt to appease the voice that kept badgering me. I'd had a couple of conversations with a roommate who assured me that my friend, Stefan, was almost never around, but that I was very welcome to come visit and stay. The roommate's name was Heinrich, and I didn't know it then, but we would become good friends. No, I wouldn't go out with him, despite his gentle hints, but we spent a lot of time together during my stay in Berlin.

Meanwhile, the driver of the snazzy car and I crossed into East Germany without incident, and he began to explain the process of crossing into West Berlin. It probably helped quite a bit that he was familiar with this route, perhaps even somewhat familiar to those at the checkpoints, and that he knew the drill. While waiting in a line of cars for our turn at the border crossing into West Berlin, he told me how much it cost to cross (there wasn't a fee to cross into any other country, but here East Germany had found a money-maker), and he explained that this had to be paid in West German marks, a nice, valuable, and steady currency. I didn't have any German marks because I'd started my day in Switzerland. He agreed to accept my American dollars in exchange for some German marks. Without his helpfulness and knowledge, I'm not sure that I could have gotten across the border. At least not that night, and not if I'd been on foot.

He helped me fill out the bit of required paperwork, and we each presented our paper and passport to the guard when it was our turn. It was surprisingly easy, really, and I felt such relief to be past the border crossing and to be making my way, at last, into the walled city of West Berlin.

It was overcast and nighttime, the rain falling steadily on the city as we passed through the barbed wire and walls.

"It's so beautiful," I exclaimed, surprised by how excited I was to be there and by how great the city looked to me. I wasn't more surprised, though, than the man driving the car.

"No, it's awful here. This is the worst part. It's really ugly here."

"No, I think it's beautiful. What an amazing city."

"No, it's a great city, but parts of it like this are really ugly. This was one of those places that was heavily bombed during the war, and much of that hasn't been rebuilt yet. Yes, there are great parts of the city, nice buildings and museums and parks, but this is one of the worst parts."

I suddenly realized that I wasn't seeing the city as it truly was. I wasn't about to try to explain what I saw to this helpful stranger, but I was seeing an overlay of the old, pre-war Berlin as I gazed about. Sure I could see the buildings in front of me, but gaps were filled in with this city's old, pre-war grandeur. At times, even the buildings left fully standing seemed gauzed over by more perfect versions of themselves. My German had been improving steadily since I'd spoken with the truck driver the day before. I was understanding more German than I knew or had any right to be able to interpret, I was able to follow more German than I'd ever studied, and I was seeing the city, in stunning glimpses, as it had once been. I felt moved to be in this beautiful, grand, cosmopolitan center of science and philosophy and culture, this capital (former capital at that time, since the capital of West Germany had been moved, logically, into West Germany, to Bonn) of learning and the arts. I didn't understand how or why, but I felt that I had returned home.

Uncharted Waters

I had given my final driver the address in Kreuzberg, near Checkpoint Charlie, where the guy I'd met on the island of Santorini lived. Kreuzberg was right next to the wall that separated East and West Berlin, a largely unrestored neighborhood on the outskirts of the more built up and renovated center of the city. It was a popular neighborhood with artists, full of the trendy punk style of the 80's, and we pulled up in front of a worn building and rang the buzzer at the front door, standing, finally, in the rain, although, mind you, it was only a light drizzle. I guess that now that I had made it to my destination, the Weather Gods had gone on coffee break.

The guy who had been so helpful to me at border crossings had thrown out a few small, indirect hints, bits of flirtation, in case I might be interested in spending more time with him. "Schöne Leute haben viel Glück," he smiled at me, a last ditch effort at charming me.

"I never heard that saying before," I responded. "Are good-looking people luckier? I don't know. That's a new one. Thank you so, so much for the ride." He smiled again. Message received. Over and out.

He wasn't pushy or rude at all. I'm not complaining about this man who got me past barbed wire, guns, dogs on leashes, and guards carrying big guns. There were a lot of guns. There were floodlights and coils of barbed wire. Did I mention the guns? It was an intimidating place to cross, and I was really appreciative of his help. I'm just finishing up the story.

At the end of my three-day journey it was nighttime and, as I mentioned, it was, finally, raining, not just atmospherically, but on me. We stood there on the doorstep for a few moments and then he said, "Here, I have an idea. He pulled a little something out of his pocket and quickly proceeded to pick the lock to the building. We stepped into the dry entryway, and I thanked him again. He wished me well and headed on to destinations of his own. I can't prove it, but I think that in this walled and heavily monitored and policed city patrolled by the English, French, and Americans, I had met a spy. Whether true or not, I had been delivered safely to Berlin.

Stowaway

I sat in front of the door to the apartment, reading the book I still had with me (despite my limited possessions, I always allowed myself to carry one or two books to read and trade), tired from long days of uncertainty and stormy weather at sea, when Heinrich came around the corner. He smiled at me and welcomed me in, friends immediately, and we began to settle into our new routine as roommates. He showed me my friend's room and told me to make myself at home and to stay as long as I liked. "He's not home often. He has a lot of girlfriends. I'd leave that part of your relationship with him in the past, if I were you," he advised me, laughing. Since I hadn't come to Berlin to try to win this guy or to try to develop our up-to-this-time limited relationship, I wasn't disappointed, although I can't claim to have fully followed his advice. After putting away my few things, Heinrich and I visited for a while, and then I settled in and fell sound asleep.

In the morning my friend, Stefan, stopped by his place to shower and change and get ready to head to the university. He seemed unsurprised to see me. "You can come with me to the university, if you like. Maybe you'd like to see it?"

Stefan was completely relaxed about the American he really didn't know that well who had arrived, uninvited, to stay for an indeterminate period of time, and who had decided to sleep in his room. It turned out to be a workable arrangement since he usually came home, on the days when he returned to the apartment, from wherever he had spent the night, around the time I was having breakfast, sometimes took a little nap, and then headed out about his business. The arrangement seemed acceptable to him, and we settled into a routine, however unusual.

"Sure, I'd love to see the university," I told him. The Frei Universität, or the "Free University," was known as F. U., which, in the immaturity of my 20's, struck me as hopelessly funny. We headed to the nearby subway stop where Stefan taught me that it was required to buy a ticket to ride the metro, but that he never did. Berlin had a sort of honor system, and he recommended that if I got caught riding it for free some day, I could deal with that issue then. Once in a while I would buy a ticket, as a sort of polite gesture to this city that had welcomed me, but in all honesty, usually not, and I never did get caught.

West Berlin was a bustling city of approximately two million people, and the subway was how most people got around. Each train was composed of several cars, and new trains came along every few minutes, which was why I was so surprised, so astounded, when we stepped into one of the full, rush-hour cars, grabbed hold of the bars around us, and then I looked up as the train started to move, laughed, and greeted the man standing in front of me.

"Hi, Otto," I exclaimed. Otto was one of the three people I'd ever met and spoken with who lived in Berlin. Stefan, with whom I was now staying, was the first. The third was Ingrid, Otto's girlfriend whom he was heading to meet at F.U. where they were both students. I'd been in Berlin for a few short hours and had already seen two out of the three people I knew, in however limited a fashion, who lived in Berlin, and I was about to see the third. Plans were in place about which I knew nothing and which I couldn't

152

begin to understand or explain.

Showing Your True Colors

Berliners (not the jelly donut, the people) I met told me of a thrift store where you could buy clothes by the kilo, something I desperately needed because a backpack doesn't hold much and Berlin was experiencing a very cold winter. Not a snowy winter, as it hadn't gotten around to snowing in Germany any more than in France, but the weather was bleak, and I needed clothes. Berlin, at least at that time, and at least to my eye, was inhabited by denizens who wore black. They wore black and leather and black leather. I began to wonder if their underwear was made of leather as well. This was a cool city. It was hip. It was trendy and fashionable and cosmopolitan.

Since I'd never had a cool day in my life, and since I was damned if I was about to start now, I dug into the piles of clothes where you bought your wardrobe by weight and came up holding things that only a dedicated and sartorially blind golfer could love. I bought green pants with little animals stitched on them. I found a pink sweater and other oddments that didn't necessarily match one another and that definitely didn't match this city garbed in black. I looked like a color-blind preppie.

I didn't blend in with my "fashion" choices, and I wasn't about to start smoking cigarettes or hash or the hand-rolled cigarettes that combined tobacco and hash that some of the young Berliners I was getting to know seemed to prefer. Guided by my angels from a young age, I'd never smoked a cigarette in my life, and I wasn't going to ignore their advice now. I wasn't interested in drugs and I almost never drank alcohol. I did, however, discover that I loved German chocolate, and a strong bond was formed. My drug of choice, and it's a powerful one, has always been sugar. I drank hot chocolate with homemade whipped cream in cafés and consumed more than my share of chocolate bars, biking my way around Berlin in winter fueled by cocoa butter and milk fat.

I bought bright clothes and steered clear of drugs partly because I can be stubborn, partly because I don't like to go with the crowd, and largely because I had been trained by my father to think and act for myself, to never try to fit in, and to deliberately not go along with the group. "Don't be a sheep! You're not a follower! 'Everyone else is doing it' is usually the worst reason to do something. People end up doing very stupid things when they think like that. Just look at Nazi Germany. They followed a madman to their own destruction!"

This might be a good time to mention that my father is Jewish. He had uncles who had escaped from Vienna and Italy. Barely. He had professors, family, and friends who had escaped from Europe or had survived unimaginable years in camps with horrific stories to tell. We didn't know the stories of those who hadn't fled, who hadn't survived.

"Oy," my grandfather groaned to me when I called to let G & G know, briefly, because international calls were pricey, where I was. "Germany? Does it have to be Germany? What are you doing in Germany? Why?"

I felt bad, I truly did, but unaccountably, I also knew that I was exactly where I was supposed to be, and stranger still, I felt at home and at peace.

Right now, though, I was in my first full day in Berlin riding in a subway car, catching up with Otto, a man I'd met on a flight in Europe that past summer. He'd been traveling on vacation with his girlfriend, Ingrid. During our shared flight they'd told me about what they studied at the university in Berlin. We'd had a great visit on the plane, the last leg of my trip from the States. We'd chatted a bit further at the luggage carousel, and then I'd wished them a great trip. Now I was about to see Ingrid again. West Berlin was a city of two million people. This made no sense. Impossible coincidences, strange happenings, and synchronistic events were typical of my entire stay in Berlin.

Albatross

One early morning that December in Berlin I had a terrible dream in which I saw a giant white jet flying through the air. On its side, written in enormous letters, were the words "Pan Am."

"There's a giant Pan Am jet flying through the sky," I thought to myself during the dream as I watched the plane fly smoothly through the air. I had barely completed that thought when the plane suddenly exploded in my mind, coming apart in some big chunks and a whole bunch of much smaller pieces as the plane disintegrated, loudly, into various bits, blown to smithereens by a bomb. It was a dream, but I knew with certainty that I'd just seen a plane blown up by a bomb. The explosion that I saw in the field of vision in my mind, while dreaming, was catastrophic—absolutely sudden and truly huge.

"Oh my God, oh my God, oh my God! Don't fly Pan Am! Whatever you do, don't fly Pan Am!" That emphatic thought was ringing in my mind over and over again as I sat up in bed now thoroughly awake and utterly horrified. "Don't fly Pan Am!"

One year later, perhaps to the day, perhaps a year and a day or two later, I was walking down the street after having returned to the States when I abruptly stopped in my tracks, my forward momentum arrested by the headlines of the front page displayed in a newspaper box on a street corner. I stood transfixed as I stared at the headlines, trying to make sense of the horrible words and photograph, a photo that seemed strangely familiar to my mind, a picture of a piece of plane wreckage from a Pan Am plane. The newspaper announced something along the lines of "Pan Am jet explodes over Lockerbie, Scotland!" I just stood there staring at those appalling, yet familiar, words through the plastic cover of the newspaper box. I couldn't bring myself to buy a paper. I was just too shocked. This was the scene that I had seen in my dream the year before. This was precisely what I had been shown. And the plane, heading to New York, had taken off from, wait for it, Germany. It had taken off from Frankfurt, stopped in London, and was then on its way to New York.

I asked my guides why they would help me hitchhike across a swath of Europe as a young, single woman–surely a risky enterprise if there ever were one, but they wouldn't let me fly Pan Am, even a year before the tragedy occurred. The answer I received was pretty straightforward.

"First of all, we can keep you safe, almost without exception, while you're on the ground if you're following our guidance very carefully. However, if you get into a plane that's going to be blown up, there's nothing we can do for you. We have no way to protect you. We can't remove you from the plane and deposit you safely back on the ground. If you're on a plane that's going to be blown up, you're going to die along with the other passengers and crew."

"I can't be the only one you warned about flying Pan Am before the explosion happened."

"Of course you weren't. Some of the people we warned listened, and some didn't. Some heard us, and others just thought it was their imagination showing them a negative scene out of their subconscious or whatever explanation they gave to the warnings they were receiving but not listening to or not understanding or not willing to heed."

"Are there some people you didn't warn?"

"We want to help and protect and guide everyone. However, many people are not paying attention to us and are too closed to receive what we're sending out, even if they claim to be extremely religious or spiritual people. If what they believe doesn't allow for guidance or messages from sources they can't see, they might not accept what they hear, see, or feel no matter how clearly we convey information that could be helpful to them."

"We transmit information in many different ways. Some people can hear or receive one way better than another. That used to be true for you as well. You were much better at hearing than at seeing. Now you can receive through a range of channels. You're developing, and as a result we're able to help you more effectively and in more ways."

They were chatty today. I wasn't going to miss the opportunity to keep asking questions.

"Is dying bad?"

"No, it's not a bad thing at all. It's all part of the larger plan, and the plan is good and loving; every life has a purpose and each lifetime needs to be completed in some fashion. The plan is safe and it is kind. People live for a time, have a range of experiences, make some good choices and some poor ones, perhaps gain some wisdom and compassion, and then they depart their bodies and return to what you might think of as the 'spirit realm.' There aren't many entrance strategies for how to show up in a human lifetime. Modern science has added variations such as in vitro fertilization and surrogates to carry babies, but there just aren't too many options beyond being born to someone or taking the slightly indirect route of adoption to arrive at one's family."

"Dying, however, is a completely different matter. The list of ways to die is long, and some people truly get creative in this regard. It doesn't ultimately matter, though. The body is exited but the life and one's consciousness continue uninterrupted as one moves on to undergo other forms of life, awareness, and experience."

"We've got work for you to do during this lifetime, work you have agreed to do, so we're going to try to help you live long enough and have what you need to get the job done. We want to help you arrive where you need to be and meet other people with whom you're meant to work until your tasks are complete."

"Thank you for that."

"You're welcome. The other part of why we gave you the dream is because we could see that there was a very high probability of a bomb being placed on a Pan Am jet on a flight from Germany to New York, which was the route you were most likely to take, but the people working to place the bomb needed time to get prepared and didn't know exactly when, how, and where they could or would do it. The details were still forming, so we thought it was just better to warn you off flying that carrier altogether. 'Better safe than sorry,' as we've heard you say."

"What about the other people who were on that flight or who could have been on that flight? What about their safety?"

"For some of them, it really was their time to go.

For others, again, they just haven't developed the ability to listen and follow guidance from us yet, so there was no way to protect them. Some of the people we warned then changed their plans in one way or another. Some people decided to travel somewhere else, or on a different day, or by another method. For others, something more interesting came up. A couple of people didn't feel well enough to travel."

"We have lots of tricks up our sleeves. We can give people car trouble on the way to the airport, have their ride run out of gas or get lost, or create some other kind of obstacle. Sometimes, though, we try and try and the individual obstinately doesn't receive our messages, gets a feeling he shouldn't travel but does so anyway, or is determined to proceed with the plans he has made regardless of any promptings or interference from us; he might proceed with the arrangements he's made even though he has a strong intuition that he shouldn't. People who think that their own plan is better than ours can be very difficult to assist." I couldn't help but take that last comment rather personally.

On this early morning in Berlin in December of 1987, a full year before the explosion actually occurred, all I knew as I lay in bed sweating from the horrible images I'd just seen in my dream was that there was no way I was going to board a Pan Am jet–ever! The dream had clearly been a warning. It had been so real. I got the message loud and clear: "Don't fly Pan Am!"

That sounds like it was probably really easy to do. Of course, after terrorists exploded a bomb in the plane over Lockerbie a year later, the Pan Am airlines went bankrupt. It was no more. No one was going to be flying Pan Am after that. However, a year earlier, while living in Berlin, a city or, to be more precise, half a city marooned like an island in the Soviet Bloc, it was a bit trickier to get in and out of West Berlin. I'd already experienced that, complete with miracles, first hand. Yes, some people drove, but many others flew. It was just really easy to hop on a plane in West Berlin in those days, especially if your destination was somewhere else in West Germany or in Western Europe. The flights were typically inexpensive within Europe, and Pan Am was usually cheaper to fly than the German carrier, Lufthansa.

My chances of flying Pan Am within Europe and to eventually use it to return back to the States were actually really high. I told my roommates about my dream. They replied in similar ways to the other people I had tried to tell about my psychic experiences in the past. "That's a crazy dream," or "That's weird," or "You're so funny," or something else along those lines were their typical responses.

Heinrich was going to a big party for New Year's Eve in Bonn. "Everyone will be there! It's going to be huge. I've got some friends going. You can stay with us."

"That sounds fun. How are you getting there," I asked?

"We're flying."

"Which airlines?"

"Pan Am."

"No thanks. I had that dream, remember?"

I couldn't be talked into joining them, and I couldn't talk them out of going. Instead we made plans to meet up in southern Germany afterwards and then go skiing together.

"I'll fly there and meet you," Heinrich told me.

"How are you going to travel south?"

"I'm not sure, but I'm definitely not flying."

It turns out that the way I got there was by looking at the ride message board at the university for people who were driving south and wanted passengers to help share expenses. I rode south with three complete strangers instead. It was a bit weird, although very tame after hitchhiking, less expensive than flying, and the trip didn't set off alarm bells in my head.

The Edges of the Map

The shocked look on Ingrid's face was priceless as we walked into the cafeteria where she was waiting for her boyfriend. The four of us visited for a bit, and then Stefan left us to take care of some things, maybe even to go to class. Ingrid and I visited for a while and exchanged addresses. She gave me her phone number as well so that we could keep in touch.

I somehow managed to lose that piece of paper containing Ingrid's address and phone number within a few days, which meant that it was going to be hard for me to find her again despite the incredible luck of my first subway ride in Berlin. I was riding the metro, probably heading over to the beautiful public library, a favorite stop of mine since coming to Berlin. The train cars were fairly full, but I'd gotten a seat and was reading a book. Coming to the end of the chapter I closed the book and looked up, taking in the scenes of Berlin outside since at the moment the train was above ground. I noticed that the person sitting directly across from me was also reading. It was Ingrid.

In all of the subway trains, each with multiple cars, coursing in and through Berlin continuously, I had been led to this precise point. I lifted one leg and reached out and tapped hers across from me. "Hi Ingrid," I said. "I lost the paper with your number on it. I'm so glad I ran into you." She started laughing, surprised to see me as well.

Apparently, at least while I was in Berlin, if the

Powers That Be wanted me to do something, go somewhere, or meet someone, I would. Ingrid and I started to get together from time to time, and when her month-long winter break came in January, she asked me if I'd like to live in her apartment while she was away on holiday. "Sure, that'd be fantastic!"

I was getting to know Berlin. I bought a bike so that I could get around easily on the bike paths that were everywhere, with their own lanes and often with their own stoplights. Since there was so little snow that season, I was able to ride wherever I needed to go as long as I dressed warmly.

I visited museums, drank cocoa in cafés, listened to music, and walked around the lakes and parks. I roamed the city streets, my view shifting periodically between how the city used to be and what it actually looked like now.

The wall that encircled West Berlin, making it an island within East Germany, was a constant reminder of where I was. It was decorated with graffiti pretty much everywhere, turning this ugly Cold War landmark into a public art space, an expanse for stream-of-consciousness musings and political commentary. At the same time, I could feel, so strongly, that this era was ending, even though I didn't hear anyone else talking about the wall coming down; it wasn't in the papers, and the people I knew didn't think it likely at all. But I knew, saw, and felt with clarity that the wall wouldn't be up much longer; I was certain of it. I walked and rode around the streets of Berlin feeling oddly free, enjoying this highly policed, and therefore ironically safe, cosmopolitan world city, thinking to myself, "When I lived in Berlin the wall was still up."

Casting Off

When Ingrid returned from her winter break, I moved into a giant apartment with seven or eight other people–it was actually hard to keep track of everyone. This place, like Ingrid's apartment, was in the rather tony Schöneberg neighborhood. The rooms were big with large windows. The ceilings seemed impossibly high, and yet there was only one bathroom. The solution created by the Germans I lived with was to never lock the door of the bathroom. One person would be on the can, someone else in the bath, and a third person might be brushing his teeth. My solution was to bathe and use the bathroom in the middle of the night. That, and to lock the door. One of my jokes, while living in Berlin in winter, was to say, "Look, there's someone with clothes on!" I found it very funny. Most other people didn't seem to get it. "What's funny about someone wearing clothes? Is it funny to walk around without them? I don't get it."

You can take the American out of the suburbs, but perhaps not suburbia out of the girl. While living in Berlin, I was often shocked.

"Heinrich, the phone is for you."

"Can you bring me the phone?"

"But you're in the bathtub?"

"Oh my God. Who cares! Just please bring me the

phone!" I'd walk into the bathroom (in that apartment the toilet and the tub had separate compartments) holding the phone out in front of me as far as my arm would reach, my eyes scanning the ceiling off to my side.

"Oh my God. You're ridiculous!"

I never managed to quite fit in, with my bright clothing, with my dislike of drugs and cigarettes, with my discomfort with pooping while people streamed in and out of a communal bathroom, but I loved the city and my time there. I might have been a fish out of water, but I was a happy little critter nonetheless. I wasn't much of a "grouper." Probably more of a flounder, I guess.

Eventually, the inevitable happened: I was running out of money. I'd tried to get jobs, but it would be me, the puny American, versus 25 Kurdish women who looked like they could bench press 100 pounds without breaking a sweat. We'd all show up for the same cleaning job. Not surprisingly, I was never hired.

I'd given my father Power of Attorney over my bank account before I left the States, so I asked him if he could wire me some of my money. He obliged and sent me $200. This was enough money for me to survive for a while longer, but certainly not enough to continue to live in Berlin while I wrapped up my time there and then purchase a plane ticket to the States.

Finally, my money had truly and finally run out. I'd gotten my father to send me some more of my money, but again, despite my request, he wouldn't send me enough to stay longer in Berlin. He didn't even send me enough to fly back to the States. I received enough of my money from home to stay another week and to buy a one-way ticket within Europe. I decided that I would leave Germany, crash with friends in other European climes, and then ask for enough money (still my money we're talking about here) so that I could return home.

I needed to buy a plane ticket but Lufthansa was too pricey and Pan Am was off limits, so I bought a ticket departing from East Berlin on one of the Eastern European carriers. It was definitely less expensive, and it wasn't Pan Am. I was set.

The evening before leaving town, I gave a big party to say good-bye and to thank everyone. I bought a bunch of food and cooked up a storm, and everything turned out surprisingly well. It was the 80's, and maybe the Germans had never had guacamole before, or maybe it was just the best guacamole ever, or maybe they just showed up ready for dinner, but that big bowl of guac was consumed, quickly, down to the slightest smear. I don't remember everything I made, I think there was chicken and potatoes too, but I guess I was trying to do "American," at least as I understood it, because there was also a large plate of brownies and other typical Americana. We had a great time, ate everything I'd prepared, and visited late into the night. In the morning a couple of friends showed up to see me off as I headed off for the bus that was going to take me into East Berlin and to the airport there. They surprised me by giving me $100 in cash–a large sum, especially then, and especially for two students. I was so touched by their generosity! "We know that you're broke," they told me. We just wanted to make things a little easier for you."

"Thank you so much!" I couldn't believe the warmth, kindness, and welcome I'd experienced during my time in Berlin. These were two American students doing a year abroad, but it didn't matter if the people I met were American, German, Turkish or whatever; with the rare exception of a few racists, the occasional Nazi clinging to a

171

dead dream of racial superiority, or the odd jerk you can meet anywhere, the people were lovely. I felt like I'd healed something inside me, something that I'd harbored, that was partly mine and partly ancestral, of the pain of the pogroms in Eastern Europe which my ancestors had fled to save their sanity and their lives, in some cases with only the clothes on their backs, and the pain, lived by various members of my family and their friends, during the war.

Yes, there was still unresolved pain in me around that familial and historical chapter, bits of anger, some disbelief, but the big knot I'd carried about from childhood had largely dissolved. Another chunk of it was faced and released a couple of days before I left town, when I finally headed to East Berlin so that when people asked me about my trip I wouldn't have to say that I had never even visited East Berlin once during all of the months of my stay in West Berlin, a short hop beyond a wall, German Shepherds, barbed wire, guns, and snipers.

Knowing the Ropes

As my time in West Berlin, a city which I'd absolutely come to love, drew to a close, I began to ask myself and my guides why I'd been sent there, and why I'd been sent there so insistently, and towards the end, in such a hurry. Part of me wonders whether the infatuated French woman who had been following me around in Annecy and had finally moved into the bed next to mine from which to get an unobstructed view of my sleeping form was about to demonstrate her crazy side, of which there clearly was one–something wasn't quite right about her eyes–and jump me or attack me or something. Maybe, but probably not.

A more likely idea that seemed to have been an important part of my going to live with Heinrich and Stefan for a time at the beginning of my Berlin adventures probably had to do with Heinrich. I wouldn't date him, but we became friends, did things together like my disastrous attempt at skiing in the high Alps which were experiencing very little snow that year, and talking and talking. His mother had died about a year before, and they had been very close. Heinrich was depressed and spoke to me periodically about how he had more than once considered killing himself over the preceding year and that those thoughts still troubled him. I like to think that having a roommate, moi, who literally had nothing to do all day, helped him have the company, the companion, the listener, to help him voice and start to let go of some of his sense of loss, and to support him in moving forward again despite not quite knowing how to go about it, without his mum. Perhaps his mother sent me to be a friend and to see him through some of the darker stages of his grief. Helping Heinrich choose to live felt like part of why I was there, but, of course, I certainly can't prove it.

I've noticed, though, that Spirit is efficient. It seems to enjoy accomplishing several tasks at once. At times the angels remind me of times when I'll call up my husband and say something along the lines of, "While you're in town, would you gas up the car, pick up a prescription, and since you'll already be at the store, grab some eggs and cream?" Spirit seems to favor a multi-tasking approach.

Yes, I was led to get out of France when there wasn't going to be a job; yes, I may have gone to Berlin to help a young man decide to push forward through this challenging time in his life; yes, I had healed a part of myself that was still stuck in a sort of painful cycle left over from World War Two; and yes, I was tutored, in a rather stringent way, to deepen my abilities to listen, to follow, and to trust in the guidance that wanted to play a central, dominant role in my life.

I'd also met wonderful people, fallen in love with a city, and matured a bit. I had learned that no matter what I wanted to believe in or not believe in, no matter how I clung to the remaining shards of a more conventional belief system, Spirit wasn't done. There was always more.

I'd turn a corner and discover that another belief of mine was about to bite the dust. I'd make a plan and discover that there was plenty more to let go of in terms of what I thought I knew and what I believed I understood. Another chance always appeared to bring me to my knees, speechless and in awe; there were always more miracles waiting. If I were willing to allow for greater guidance and spiritual connection, my life would be weirder and more miraculous and just plain old more interesting than any trajectory I could set for myself.

I had followed an insistent and unseen voice to Berlin thinking, "Well, at least I'm not one of those kooks who believes in reincarnation. That would be really crazy. Thank God I'm not one of them." I've learned, though, that as soon as I get really certain about what is and isn't possible, a blow to my carefully protected belief system is on its way.

Stilled Waters

Two days before my departure from West Berlin, one of my many roommates in the high-ceilinged, one-bathroomed apartment lent me a map of East Berlin to use for the day. Another roommate told me of the wonderful museum I just had to visit. A third friend explained to me, as a couple of people already had, that while you had to convert 25 West German marks into 25 East German marks, one-for-one, for the day in order to enter the city, those East German marks were essentially worthless.

"There's no point in bringing them back. Even if you had time to go to East Berlin again for another visit, you'd still have to exchange another 25 West German marks for the same number of East German marks."

"They're impossible to spend," I was told. "I usually buy up a bunch of books to read. You could get Goethe and Thomas Mann to read in German," another person explained.

"We both know I couldn't. I can barely get through the grocery store in German." "Grocery store" in German is Lebensmittelgeschäft. This word, a combination of three words strung together, makes it, actually, a rather short word by German standards, although it has to be capitalized because it's a noun and German nouns are always capitalized. Are they kidding? The noun is often different in the plural from its singular form. It's as if the word "car" in English became "cärne" in the plural, say, if you wanted

177

to say "two cars" or, in my completely made up German, "zwei Cärne." The endings of nouns and adjectives change depending upon whether or not they're hanging out together, which of the three genders they are, and on whether or not they're a subject, in the possessive, or a direct or indirect object at the moment. German wasn't easy. Mark Twain wrote a brilliant and hysterically funny piece called "The Awful German Language," and I couldn't write a description of my linguistic trials with German that was one tenth as clever or witty, so I'll leave it to his capable storytelling to explain just why the German language is a beast.

I love books, but no, I wouldn't be buying any books in German to unsuccessfully stuff into my overloaded backpack. I'd already held a giant giveaway of the things that I'd accumulated during my stay in Berlin. I don't remember my clothes being hot ticket items, but maybe they were accepted to be polite or the way one might put a bright pillow in an otherwise drab living room, as a sort of "accent piece."

"I usually go to the theater in East Berlin," someone told me. They have some really good, classic performances there. You'll come home late, but it's fun and a good way to get rid of some extra cash."

"Maybe. That might work," but I secretly doubted that I'd be up for a late evening. I didn't mind going to the theater by myself, doing things by myself was a well-established pattern in my life, but I had a party to shop and cook for the next day.

"We'll see. I'll figure something out."

I stuffed the map into my day bag without reading it over. I'd figure out where I was and where to go when I got there. Usually, when in a new town, I just liked to wander around, at least at first, letting my feet lead me where they wanted, taking in the sights and soaking up the feel of a new place.

I got up early and took the subway from West Berlin to the stop in central East Berlin where you could disembark, go through a passport control, and hand over your strong West German currency. A bunch of other tourists and visitors coming in for the day exited the train as well. I had my papers examined, exchanged my 25 marks, and started out of the station and into the city, the other "half" of the same city I'd been living in for a few months. The people turned toward the center of town, a logical choice for their visit. Not particularly surprisingly, I turned the other way, walking away from the crowd. I'd only gone a short distance, maybe two or three blocks, when, after turning a corner, I heard, very distinctly and firmly, perhaps even with a bit of an exasperated tone to the voice, "You're going the wrong way!"

"How can I possibly be going the wrong way?" I exclaimed rather loudly, yet silently, in my head.

"I'm not going anywhere. I have the entire day to wander around this walled city. It's impossible to get too lost. It has a high, guarded wall all around it. When in doubt, head away from the wall. If I'm stuck, I can ask someone for directions. Oh, and I have a map of the city in my bag. There's no problem here. I don't have any destination in mind at all."

"You're going the wrong way."

"Okay. Fine." I turned around and headed the other way up the street. "Apparently I'm going somewhere. Apparently there's a right and a wrong way to meander through a city."

About halfway up the street I began to shake. "Oh my God, oh my God, there's a synagogue here!" I could feel its presence so strongly. I couldn't see it, but I was shaking more and more. I found a stoop to sit on, reached into my bag and pulled out the map I'd been given. I hadn't thought I'd need it at all. Instead, I'd only been in town for a few minutes and already felt a desperate need for the tangible, non-negotiable "truth" of a map.

Starboard

As I unfolded the map I looked up toward the street sign ahead so that I could know which road I was on and what the cross street was. That's how completely I hadn't cared where I was.

I found the names of the two streets and then looked at the map, toward the center of town, using the train station I'd recently exited to help me get my bearings. I found the street where I was sitting on a step, shaking. I moved my hand along the street to the place where it intersected with the name up the road. My hand traced that street a bit to the right, knowing, somehow, that my destination, chosen by Spirit, was off to the right, and my finger stopped at the Star of David there marking an old synagogue.

With trepidation I stood up and headed for the intersection. Unwilling to commit to turning the corner, I craned my neck around the edge of the building. Yes, I could see it further down and across the way. I gathered up my courage, turned the corner, and walked to stand facing the synagogue. It was tall. It was stone. It was burnt.

I dissolved into tears. I cried and cried from the depths of my being and I knew, somehow, that I had witnessed this tragedy, in another lifetime, in a past lifetime, which was something that I didn't believe in. I knew that I had been a man and that during that time in November of 1938 known in German as Kristallnacht, and in English, often, as The Night of Broken Glass, I'd realized that Jews were going to be attacked and killed, their lives destroyed. On Kristallnacht, Nazis broke windows in shops and homes owned by Jews, stealing from them during the rampage. They destroyed synagogues, taking their archival information from them first, information that could be helpful in identifying Jews in their communities. About 100 Jews were killed that night and many, many more were injured in Germany and in parts of Austria and Czechoslovakia.

In that lifetime I'd lost property during Kristallnacht, as had people I cared about, both through its destruction and its theft. I'd lost people I'd cared about that night and in the chaotic, destructive, vicious times that ensued. On that night in 1938 I'd realized that my way of life was truly over and personally observed people behaving with great cruelly toward others.

This synagogue had been kept as a memorial, as a testament, to those atrocities, as a reminder of the past and of wrongs committed in full view of, and often with the willing help, of ordinary citizens.

"Never follow. You have to think for yourself. You have to be your own person. That takes courage. It can be lonely. It's the only way to be a good and authentic person. Be yourself. Have the courage to stand up. Have the courage to stand alone." Words like these had been absorbed by me as my father tried to teach me to be a good human being, growing up years later in the United States. But he knew people. He understood the good and the bad of which they were capable and how right action could be the harder, riskier choice.

Other people walked by, staring at me with stricken looks on their faces. I was a mess. For the others on the street at that time, the synagogue was a place they passed by often, perhaps. They glanced its way for a moment, but moved on. A few tourists lingered for a bit, the winds and waters stilled, the air silent as their trajectories paused in the wake of the massive, silent building encrusted with weathered carbon from the old fire, and then they moved on too, other sights to see, other things to do that day. I knew that I didn't have anywhere else I needed to be. I had come to East Berlin to witness this dead edifice in front of me and to honor what it marked.

After a while, spent, I rubbed my eyes and my face and moved on. The voices were silent as I headed to the center of town. I saw a large square. "I was killed there. That's where I died." That thought emerged in my head as I crossed the plaza.

I visited a museum with important works on its walls. Normally I love museums, and this was a grand place, but today I couldn't name a single work I saw as I made my way through its collection, resting periodically to gaze a bit longer here and there. But I was numb. I was visiting the museum because it was there, because one was supposed to, because I remembered, in the back of my mind, that visiting museums was something I really liked to do.

After the museum I bought myself an ice cream from some sort of vendor. Other people were eating ice cream, so I thought that I should try one too. I'd been in East Berlin for about three hours, and all I'd purchased so far was an entrance ticket to a museum. I needed to get to work if I was to have any chance of getting through the enormous sum of 25 East German marks that day.

I managed to eat about three bites of the ice cream before I started to feel queasy. It tasted lousy, a bit like ice milk, low quality ice milk, that is, but definitely not ice cream. I'm someone known for eating whatever is put in front of me. "Kids are starving," I'd heard growing up. "This is not a restaurant. Don't be picky. Eat your food." These were all common refrains during mealtimes when dissent was uttered, perhaps at the appearance of a beautifully cooked beef tongue pointing, in all its glory, in my general direction from its place of honor on the dinner table.

Mom hadn't spoken of it much, but I knew that she and her family had often been hungry during the war. It's hard to be hungry, especially as a child or as the parents of children who are just too thin, a sight my grandparents would have had to face. My mother had recounted hearing people go through the streets crying out "I'm hungry" as they made their way, desperately, through the streets to wherever it was that they would finally stop and likely die. Another dead from hunger. My family was among the luckier ones. People would stop at their front door, a fine home on a nice street, begging for food, my grandmother giving them tea with honey, nothing more to be spared. People died from hunger all over Europe during the war, and there was plenty of famine to go around–it was a war, after all.

But today I just couldn't eat it. I dumped it into the trash and resumed my tour through this Germany I hadn't glimpsed since the moment I'd crossed the border into West Berlin months before in the rainy dark. I'd enjoyed modern West Berlin, a walled city, a militarized city, perhaps, but one of culture, of beautiful public buildings, of lakes and country homes, of music and cafés.

I lived in modern West Berlin with an overlay of pre-war Berlin in my mind, showing itself to me regularly. I could see and feel the beauty of the old city, enjoy the architecture that no longer existed, sense its pride in being an intellectual and artistic center for all of Europe. Why stop there? For the world. Weirder still, I knew my way around. I couldn't get lost. Once in a while, it's true, a street I was walking on, confidently, would stop further down, interrupted by the wall, and I'd have to redirect myself, but I couldn't get lost. I knew where I was instinctively, and where I was was at home.

Now, though, I was in East Berlin, the poor twin, mostly unrepaired and unrenovated, a Soviet city in the heart of East Germany, home to many soldiers and the ever-present East German police, the Stasi, of which one in three East Germans was a member according to a post-Cold War estimate I read after the wall came down in the fall of 1989, a year and a bit after I'd left the city. This was early spring in 1988. Everyone was spying on everyone else, it turned out, in East Berlin in those days. It was a sad place, a depressed and dreary town, and everywhere I looked I saw the war and its echoes.

I left the center and began to wander again, walking straight to the Jewish cemetery, a place I hadn't known existed. Not surprisingly, there didn't seem to be any other tourists there. I had entered the East Berlin of ordinary people going about their lives, but I'd done it with a sense of direction and purpose. There was a theme here, and it wasn't subtle. I was on a tour of old Jewish Berlin. I was in the neighborhood where I felt I'd lived before the start of World War Two. In fact, I was walking down a street I was sure I'd once known well, one where I'd had a little shop. I'd lived in an apartment with high ceilings nearby. I had been married. I'd had children.

Had they made it to Argentina with the children of other families that we'd sent there, a group of us, pooling our resources, with a few adults to keep watch over them? I thought so. That would have already happened. That was after the yellow star and marks and graffiti went up on the wall of my shop. It was before Kristallnacht, before I joined the resistance, before I was killed, very quickly, really, a traitor in the midst of our little, fledgling resistance ratting us out. Had the war even officially started yet? It was a bit blurry, but I knew where I was standing when I'd been killed, and I felt the sadness, the hopelessness, the certainty of death, and the tyranny, oppression, and injustice of that time.

I walked into a café populated mostly by men having a drink to punctuate their day, and ordered some tea. I then found a little shop that sold books where I bought some postcards. I think I tried to eat something else, but that didn't work either. Finally, I decided, I've seen it. I've walked the city and seen the museum and some of the grander boulevards, like Unter den Linden, and I'd taken all I could take of this city too populated by a sad and ghostly past for me.

I was making my way back to the train station, not at all surprised to know exactly which way to head, when I remembered all of the East German money I was carrying in my pocket. I was walking down a quiet street when a shabbily dressed man stepped out of a smaller intersecting street in front of me.

I reached out and gave him a large handful of money saying, "Ich brauche das nicht." "I don't need this," my attempt at German told him as our eyes met, his face astonished, but also scared. He nodded and quickly headed off in another direction, putting some distance between himself and me, not looking back, the money already hidden away in the folds of his clothes.

"Well that was easy," I thought, as every single thing I was carrying was carefully turned over, opened, emptied, and examined by an angry guard who didn't seem to like the fact that I was American. I tried my German on him to make a bit of peace, but he wasn't the peaceful sort and my German wasn't the sort to bring smiles to faces, that is, unless they were chuckling at my bungled efforts. Yes, I understood more German that I had any right to. And yes, I could make myself understood when needed, but it was still a difficult language and actual study would be required if I were ever going to learn it properly.

"That was really easy." Not going through border crossings. Those weren't much fun. Spending the money– that was really easy. The trick, I realized, is not to think that you needed to spend it on yourself, or even to spend it at all. I'd simply found a person who appeared to be in need of cash, maybe in rather desperate need of cash, made sure no one was watching, and handed it all over. Mission accomplished.

The day after the good-bye party I handed over my backpack to a very thorough couple of inspectors at the airport in East Germany who went through everything in detail, even opening up a pen and rifling through my collection of tampons. I then boarded a plane that looked like it probably had a few more flights in it, given the proper encouragement. If there was such as thing as Bulgaria Air, then that was it. I thought it should have been called "Bring Your Own Epoxy Glue." Duct tape could have been helpful as well. The entire contraption shook on take off and rattled while in the air. I decided I was safe. The guides hadn't said a peep about not flying shoestring airlines running ancient aircraft. They'd told me not to fly Pan Am, and I'd listened.

After some time visiting friends in Spain, I purchased a plane ticket to cross the Atlantic and flew back to the States to resume my life there. I'd wanted to join Ingrid studying Arabic in Syria in the fall, which had sounded like an exciting idea to me, and a much worse one to my father. He called the State Department and prepared a packet for me full of travel warnings. To this day, I got that I would have been fine and that I should have gone. Oh well, I didn't listen to that guidance either and instead moved back into my old life, working at jobs I didn't much care for in a city that didn't charm or stun me with echoes of its past. It was while walking along one of its streets that I saw the headlines announcing the downed Pan Am jet that December of 1988. This, too, is where I was living when I had the experience of being engulfed in a brilliant white light.

The Ship's Log

I moved into a room in a house with a friend and his roommate. The roommate had two large and extraordinarily hairy cats. It was hot that summer, a record-breaking kind of heat, and I left the window cracked open, slept with a little fan angled right on me, and kept the door to my room open at night in search of a breeze, however scarce.

For whatever reason, these large and dandery cats immediately took to sleeping with me, the door left ajar being all of the invitation they needed. They lounged on my bed, not only with me, but on my pillow, and not only on my pillow, most mostly on top of my head. I was miserable. I liked the cats just fine, and apparently, to the consternation of my new roommate, they'd found someone new to adore and pester, but they made my attempts at getting some sleep at night, already a hot, sweaty, unpleasant effort, much more difficult. Not surprisingly, I've been allergic to cats ever since.

My life just wasn't functioning smoothly at that point, whether it be work, where I lived, or even just trying to get some sleep at night. I made mental notes of the various problems I was having in my life, but I wasn't yet willing to find a new port, switch out the crew, and find some new maps by which to chart my course.

One sweltering afternoon I was sitting on my bed, reading through a few of the books I'd kept that my family had been given a couple of years before when my brother had been diagnosed with cancer. Naturally, people don't know what to do in a situation like that, one in which a young man was staring down the possibility of death, so they gave us, big readers all, books. And not knowing what to do either, I had read them.

The Treasure Map

I sat on my bed, sweating, reading, and shooing away the occasional cat making a daytime incursion into my territory. I'd read every book we'd been given, and I'd found things of value and comfort in each of them, but the writers of the two I'd liked best, Dr. Jerry Jampolsky's *Love Is Letting Go Of Fear*, and Hugh Prather's *Notes on How to Live in the World and Still be Happy*, had both referred to another book as being their inspiration: *A Course In Miracles*.

My brother was well now, which was the biggest gift in my life. The voice had promised that he would fully recover from the cancer, and as always, it had spoken words of truth containing the promise of grace.

Grace is invisible, so you have to look for it carefully. I believe it is God's way of answering prayer, and its presence can be developed in our minds and in our lives through gratitude, kindness, and by sending blessings out into the world to those around us, to other countries, and to our fragile home, the earth itself. Grace is perhaps the most important gift that emerged Pandora's ill-famed box; grace clears our errors and it forgives our forgetting of the truth and meaning of our lives and purpose as it dissolves away pain and sorrow and loss.

My brother's illness, the books we received from friends to help us through that difficult time, and the compassion and wisdom gained by watching someone young and so close to me courageously face a life-threatening illness had, together, led to the other great gift that found me during this challenging period in my life. That gift, a map for stormy weather, white water rapids, and rocky coastlines, became central to my life then and since; I was led to the three-volume set of *A Course In Miracles* (ACIM). The language in the text was largely Christian, which made me somewhat uncomfortable at the time. Jews and Catholics, among others, were involved in its initial writing, editing, and publication, and the ideas presented often felt Buddhist to me. In the end, I decided that it was a universal teaching that went to the heart of Spirit past all labels and worldly identification.

I often didn't really understand what I was reading as I made my way through *A Course In Miracles*, which was disconcerting since I'd been accustomed to reading words and understanding them. At the same time, I always felt better as I read it so I persevered. I've been reading *A Course In Miracles* ever since, its meaning and wisdom becoming clearer and clearer to me over the years.

While sitting in the oppressive heat, the hottest summer on record for that city up until that point, I was reading through some of the workbook lessons in ACIM and had been drawn to the daily lesson entitled, "We are all among the ministers of God." I sat there rereading that lesson and thinking about it.

I'd had a number of different jobs including tutoring, teaching English as a Second Language, waitressing, working in a bookstore, secretarial work, and bartending, among others, but I'd not embarked on anything that I could describe as my career. Periodically I would wonder what I should do with my life, about what I wanted to do with my life, and about what kind of work I should really be doing.

In the past when I'd thought things like, "I could be a teacher," I'd heard something along the lines of, "Okay," in response. "That would be fine." By "being a teacher," I meant teaching in the United States rather than teaching English abroad, which was exciting but not what I wanted to continue to do.

"I could be a lawyer," I'd stated before, only to be met with:

"Do you really want to argue with people for the rest of your life? You're good at arguing. You'd win most of the time, but is that how you want to spend your life?" The voice was almost incredulous. Had I paid no attention at all to what it had been trying to teach me over the years? I was supposed to develop inner peace and learn to extend that increasing calm and stillness outward, not litigate.

"No, I'm not really interested in the law, but I don't know what to do."

I'd think of all sorts of different jobs and career options and test them out once in a while with the wiser beings in my midst. I'd get answers ranging from, "That sounds okay" to total silence. Never, not once, had I suggested a career and heard "That's perfect!" in response. Of course, I hadn't suggested the idea of "I could be a writer" to my guides, which is odd since when I was little that was what they had told me would be my profession, but I still hadn't gotten around to fulfilling that directive. I imagine the idea of "being a writer" would have been received positively. I think I've mentioned that my guides are patient with me.

Flags and Pennants

I lay the book down in my lap and looked off into the hot summer air of my bedroom, muggy, oppressive, and dense. The words I'd been reading still echoed in my mind. According to the book, *A Course in Miracles*, we are all meant to minister to one another as we go through life. That made perfect sense to me. Every day there were countless opportunities to do good, to be helpful or thoughtful, to lend a hand to someone else, and while I often didn't notice those moments, or I let them pass me by when I did, sometimes I did respond to the opportunity to "minister" to another person and the results were generally satisfying. My life felt meaningful and purposeful when I "ministered" to others.

I had grown up in a non-religious household, without a connection to scripture, church, synagogue, or a religious practice or training of any kind, so this kind of thinking, or at least, this kind of wording, was new to me. "Treat others with kindness and respect" was a familiar concept in my home growing up. The idea of "ministering" was new.

"I could be a minister," I mused to myself.

I'd imagined that I was alone in my room. Okay, I should have been past thinking that my thoughts were private by this point in my life, but most of the time words rattled around in my head unanswered. I was just sitting and reviewing some of the ideas I'd been reading about, or so I thought. Not only was I surprised by what happened next, I was astounded, exalted, stunned, and several other sorts of reason-defying emotions.

The words, "I could be a minister" passed through my mind, and the heavens opened up in my little room. An angelic host, invisible to me but really, really, really loud, burst into song all around me.

I jumped from the bed, looking around me wildly for the source of this choir of angels. I had heard of such a thing as a "choir of angels," from Christmas carols, I suppose, but up until that moment I'd believed it to be a poetic turn of phrase, not an actual fact. Now I knew otherwise.

Invisible angels bursting into song all around me was a different sort of answer to the question "What should I do with my life?" from any I'd ever received before, and I hadn't been asking a question at all, or at least I hadn't realized that I was.

I couldn't imagine a more emphatic "Yes" in response to any question. It was certainly the most resounding "yes" I'd ever heard or heard of.

Now I knew beyond a shadow of a doubt that the songs I'd sung as a child were speaking of an actual choir, one that it was possible to hear, if perhaps infrequently, when something higher than oneself really wanted to make its feelings about a subject known.

The only person I told about that experience at the time was a good friend of mine whose father was a minister, an actual minister of a mainstream church.

My friend, as was perhaps his predisposition, was very happy for me to have received, as I was beginning to think of it, "a call to ministry," but he was also befuddled given the fact that he knew that many members of my family were Jewish.

"So I think this is great. It's really great news, and I'm really happy for you." He didn't question the angelic choir bit for an instant, perhaps his home life having prepared him better for that sort of possibility, and he had no trouble believing that people could and did receive "calls to ministry." No, for him that was the easy part. His question to me was one I hadn't even considered.

"So, can I ask, what do you think of Jesus?"

"I don't know. I hadn't thought about it," I responded candidly, at which point he began to roll around on the floor, clutching his side and laughing hysterically. Just as "a choir of angels" had recently been proven to me to be "a thing," to actually exist, rolling on the floor in laughter was also being demonstrated as a real option in response to hilarity.

The North Star

Whereas while I was living in Berlin my life had seemed to have a natural rhythm and to flow, back in the States I was dating the absolutely wrong guy for me and had a series of jobs I really didn't like. I felt stuck. Stuck and depressed. In Berlin I was in a flow state. Now I was mired down. I moved out of the room with the fluffy cats after a serious safety issue in the neighborhood and into an apartment that turned out to be infested with cockroaches and yet still managed to be a fairly expensive place to live. In retrospect, paying anything at all for that apartment was too much, but somehow I didn't have the energy at that time to restart my life elsewhere. I think that this is why Spirit had wanted me to study in Syria–to avoid the mistakes and difficult few years I was starting to experience. My guides had tried to send me off to Santa Fe before I'd left for Europe, then they had tried to propel me to Syria rather than return to the States.

It was a peaceful Syria then, controlled by a dictator, unfortunately, but it wasn't the zone of war and horror it has become in recent years. In the 1980s the cost of living was really low, and the tuition for studying Arabic was about $60 per semester, so it was a place where I could have learned a lot and made my diminished savings stretch. Finding families who wanted their kids to learn English from an experienced tutor would probably have been pretty easy as well.

My guides threw out the idea of having me move to Syria or to Santa Fe for a little while after I'd returned to the U.S., and finally the guidance just left me to my own devices. Maybe it had just given up telling me where to go for a while since I clearly wasn't listening to or following the advice given about where to live and work and study.

Today I've finally gotten the message that it is important, essential, really, to always follow any guidance I receive. When I haven't, even with little, tiny suggestions, I've always regretted it. And the truth is, it's impossible for me to tell, in the moment, what's a little thing and what's a big thing. Even when looking back in retrospect, I don't think that I have sufficient wisdom or insight to distinguish between what is important and what is minor, what is pivotal and what is a simple moment in one's life without much of a ripple factor into the world.

During that time I felt very alone. The psychic experiences were still happening on a regular basis, although they didn't feel as fun, or whimsical, as they had while I was in Berlin–now they mostly related to parking and staying safe in a city that could get dangerous. Those promptings were helpful, but life itself just wasn't much fun.

I still didn't have anyone to talk to who understood the experiences I was having or who was having similar experiences. Perhaps if I'd grown up in liberal Berkley or in a religious community such as the Catholic Church, or in any sort of religious environment at all, I would have had a helpful background or context or at least someone to confide in. On second thought, perhaps not.

The climate in this country seems so much more open and accepting now, and there are lots of people who are openly interested in psychic phenomena, paranormal experiences, spiritual questioning and questing, and the like. Back then, though, at least among the people I knew, I was utterly alone in my experiences. I worried that I might be going crazy. Past lives. Who could take those seriously? Hearing voices and receiving guidance from beings unseen– who did that?

One day I just felt that I couldn't take it any longer; I began to pray and pray. "God, I can't take this. I feel like I'm going crazy. I don't have anyone to talk to about this. No one understands. They think it's strange. They think I'm strange. Help me. Please help me."

As I continued to pray, the prayer changed and became more specific. "Dear God, if past lives are real, if they're real and if I'm truly psychic, not crazy, if they're real and important and I'm psychic and I'm supposed to be psychic and it is your will for me to be psychic, I need a sign. I need to know for sure. Is this true and real?"

Suddenly, as I sat with my eyes closed, a brilliant white light appeared on the edge of my inner mind and came flooding toward me, enveloping me in its brilliance. I was completely encased in this whiter-than-white light except for a small area around my left elbow, which was somehow held out of the light. Other than that, I was in The Light.

Of course, at this point in my life, I'd never read about "going to the light," or other similar experiences, and of course I didn't have any friends who'd ever told me about such an experience, so I had no idea what was happening. I didn't have any previous understanding of this kind of experience, or even that it was a kind of experience that other people have had, have spoken of, and have written about.

Instead, what I knew was that I was seeing God. I

was seeing the teeny-tiniest littlest dot of what God really was, smaller than the dot made by a sharp pencil on a blank piece of paper, and that miniscule dot of God was absolutely overwhelming, totally flooding my mind and being with its brilliance. I was in awe. I was in complete and perfect awe, stunned, and utterly overwhelmed. My eyes stayed closed against the brilliant whiteness of this Light, brighter by many, many factors than any light I'd ever seen before, brighter than my mind could conceive, could imagine, could even hold. I felt like I might be dissolved into that Light but something grasped me firmly by my left elbow and kept me right where I was, as I was. I knew I was safe, but my mind, my old beliefs and sense of self, of who I was, what my life was about, what it meant, what God was, about everything– well that was all dismantled in a flash.

I was tiny. I was a dot. I was smaller than small, yet I was cared for, watched over and protected, and loved by this enormous, infinite Presence that was the All that contained everything. And that Everything was huge. My mind couldn't understand the tiniest little speck of this grandeur, the smallest little blip that could be shown to me without my being dissolved, finally, into speechless awe.

I'm not a big believer, anymore, in time and space. Physics tells us that space-time doesn't exist the way most of us think about time and space, that many parallel universes exist with us in them, simultaneously, that time can flow backwards, that life is a giant hologram, and that particles pop in and out of existence, among other concepts. I don't understand physics at all, yet I accept it as valid, evolving in its efforts to describe and explain the impossible. I've already seen that it's all one colossal whole: complex, resonant, and teeming with intelligence and knowledge so far beyond anything I could even hope to comprehend. For me, this whole is connected, meaningful and purposeful, and it is, in its fundamental essence, both conscious and kind.

Despite having had more and more psychic experiences and more and more different kinds of experiences over the years, from leaving my body (a story for another time), to entering the white Light, to hearing an angelic choir, to dreams, visions, and having voices speak to me and through me, more than ever I am forced to realize how much I don't understand and how much I don't know.

I have developed a firm belief in God, although what God really is exists so far beyond my ability to describe or fathom. Yes, God is real, all-powerful, and exists here–now–always. But actually, I really don't know anything. I don't think, as little specks of the divine, as beloved, holy, yet tiny beings experiencing human lifetimes, it's possible, in the end, to know or understand much of the greater mysteries through which we move and by which we live. I have flashes when I think I understand something of the larger picture, and then my thoughts dissolve into the impossible hugeness and complexity of it all. It's beyond me and my understanding, and I guess that's fine.

We can't really know, but what we can do is follow. We can do our best to listen and to follow and, I believe, if we're willing to obey this brilliant and loving Light, this infinite conscious presence, this Truth, our lives will be guided onto a more purposeful, joyful, and meaningful path.

Are past lives real? Well, I asked the question and I was given an answer of "YES!" But do I believe in them? No, not really.

I believe that from our human perspective of being born, having a range of different emotions and experiences, opinions and points of view, of time and of space, of some things happening first and other things happening later, of some people, trees, rivers, animals, and other stuff being over there, and of other ones occupying, as separate entities, this space over here–from that very limited and earthy framework, yes, past lives seem real to me.

Actually, though, it's all right here and right now. It's one giant wholeness, one indivisible entity. And no, I don't understand it at all except to say that from my lifetime and view point as me, an American woman living on a planet that many of us have agreed to name "Earth," from that perspective we each live separate and multiple lifetimes, time is real, and space exists. Oh, and yes, I really am psychic and I really am meant to be psychic, and it is all somehow a part of something larger, a piece in a grander plan, a plan that includes us all living through the experience of separate identities having lifetimes organized in time and space. And you're meant to be psychic too, not just once in a while, but continuously because the angels are speaking to you too; they want to help you and guide you and make your life safer and easier and more meaningful and joyful.

If we're willing to allow it, to listen deeply from a place of profound peace within, and if we're willing to open our hearts and minds to the loving wisdom with which we are surrounded, we can all be guided by angelic forces throughout our lives. Heaven can inhabit the earth if we allow it. The Kingdom of Heaven is here and now, within our innermost self, in the quiet space at our very core. What better way is there to connect to the Divine than by listening to the stillness and truth within?

A Shot Across the Bow

Six years after Gabrielle's wedding, and the weddings of some other friends, I was invited to an old prep school friend's wedding at an elegant church followed by an even more elegant reception at a club on the water. I attended the wedding alone. That was no surprise–I did lots of things alone. I was dating that wrong-for-me someone at the time, but I was trying to end the relationship, although without much success.

Before getting mired in the relationship with Randy, I'd heard, before heading out on a second date with him, "If you go out with him again you'll get stuck." I'd been clearly warned, yet I clearly hadn't listened.

Meanwhile at the wedding party I did my best to mingle and be sociable. When it was time to throw the bouquet, I joined the other single women as they settled into their bouquet-catching stance. I was twenty-seven years old, and I was tired of dating. I wanted to get married; I wanted to have kids. The voice, the one that had told me that my first husband would be taken from me, was by now almost completely forgotten. When it was time for the bouquet toss, my friend stood a little apart from her friends and gave the bouquet a good, strong backwards throw. No one else had a chance. The bouquet came zooming toward me at full bouquet velocity. Like the last time, this bouquet was headed right between my eyes. I could have caught it or been smacked by it.

I clutched the bouquet and began to shake. My friend, the new bride, came up to congratulate me. "Are you okay?" she wondered, as she assessed my trembling form. I have a feeling the happy smile that had been on my face moments earlier was gone. I didn't look like the next excited bride; I probably looked frightened or at least wary. A terrible sense of foreboding enveloped me. It was about to happen. The cycle was about to start.

The other women were giving me strange looks. I didn't know how to explain to my friend what this meant, and anyway, it was her wedding. I wasn't about to talk about my personal concerns on her big day. I remembered the first bouquet and realized that the whole sequence was about to begin. I knew that I would be marrying soon, and I also knew that it would not be to the man with whom I was jousting through a protracted break up. I held in my hands the kind reminder that even though I would lose the first one, there would be a second marriage for me, one that would be "the keeper." I continued to shake and must have looked quite startled and bewildered. A couple of people asked whether or not I might have had a bit too much too drink. I certainly must have looked unsteady on my feet. Explaining that I tended to drink little-to-none, and that this wedding was no exception to that pattern, was more information than was being asked for by the simple, "Are you all right?"

Sometimes, I thought, when the universe really wants to make sure that you understand something, it goes out of the way to render the message extremely clear. Did my guides have a flair for the dramatic or did they just enjoy metaphor?

I felt scared of my future yet comforted by the idea that at least there was a second bouquet. I would marry twice. The first time, my husband would die. The second marriage would last. Once again I had no one to whom I could tell this story. I felt quite alone and said nothing.

I guess that when you can't change your fate, the only thing to do is to face it, to stare it straight in the eye and tell the universe, "Ok, let's do this. I'm game. Batter up."

First Mate

The day I met Pete was as ordinary as they come. I was still dating Mr. Wrong-for-Me while working dead-end jobs and trying to figure out the direction my future should take, somehow still not willing to head west as I had been told.

When Pete and I would run into each other in town, we would chat a bit, a nagging feeling of familiarity inhabiting the edges of my mind even though we'd only met recently and even though we were so different in many ways.

One day he asked me for a ride, and since I had a car and he didn't, I said "sure," that I could drop him off on my way home. We were at a stoplight when he turned to me and asked, "Will you marry me?"

Okay, so first of all, that's a lousy way to propose to someone. I'm not the most romantic person, but he was pushing the outer limits of that particular convention.

Secondly, we weren't dating. I was going out with someone else, and Pete and I had never so much as held hands. His question was unexpected, illogical, irrational, and verged on the rude.

Stranger still, in response I heard myself say, "Yes."

Then I screamed. Really, I screamed out loud because I'd heard what I'd just said. I'd just said "ok" to marrying a guy I barely knew, who was perpetually broke and lived with his mother, and with whom I had very little in common.

Much later, when I thought back on how psychic Pete had been, I realized that I had been heavily manipulated on that day, and also on subsequent days, but he caught me off guard, and after years of not wanting to get married I ran splat into the man I'd been unconsciously avoiding. It seems, in retrospect, that Spirit was trying to help me not make this particular mistake and not meet this psychically powerful, manipulative guy, probably having someone else in mind for me to marry, someone, I imagine, whom I would have met if I had followed my guides' directives to where they wanted me to live.

I haven't met many professional psychics over the years since, or at least not very many genuine ones, but they will almost always tell you that they mind their own business and don't eavesdrop on other people's thoughts, that they respect boundaries and don't interfere with other people's lives or choices, and that they definitely don't use their abilities to control or influence other people. The truth is, some do, and some don't.

Pete, I would realize years later, often used his intuitive talents to help people, but even more often he used them for personal gain, for his own agenda. It had never occurred to me to try anything of the sort since I wasn't comfortable with these abilities and was only willing to use them to follow, when I did follow, the loving guidance I received and which was always designed to help and to heal. As a result, I was utterly blindsided by Pete's question and by the force of his mind invisibly intruding into my thoughts, will, and decision-making, presenting his plans and goals as my own. I wasn't wary, and I wasn't at all aware of what he was doing. He pushed into my mind to create my response and agreement to his proposal, and my mind was no longer fully my own. In fact, my mind and my thoughts wouldn't fully return to my own power and jurisdiction until after his death. I wouldn't understand the extent of the many, many ways that he had manipulated me and my thoughts and behavior, daily, until some years after he had passed away.

After agreeing to get married, I broke up with Randy, which was a relief. At least that decision was a good one. Then I went on a first date with Pete.

While eating our fast food burgers he turned to me and said, "I need to know that you'll be okay if I die. I need to know that you'll be okay and that you'll go on with your life if I die."

"What are you talking about?" I wanted to know, creepy shivers running down my back.

"I don't think I'm going to live to be very old. I've always had the feeling that I would die young, so I need to know that you're okay with that possibility and that you'll be all right and will go on with your life."

Pete's bizarre, pre-dating marriage proposal was followed by the weirdest first-date conversation I could imagine. I'd avoided getting too serious with anyone; I'd sidestepped marriage, and then fallen right into it. Hadn't I been paying attention?

Stormy Weather

It wasn't an easy marriage. I worked hard at multiple jobs. Pete worked occasionally, plagued, it turned out, by a severe work allergy. As far as I could tell, he really didn't like to work too much. He really, really didn't.

I loved him, despite his weirdness. I worked hard, and he played computer games and watched *Star Trek*. He made me laugh. He amazed me with his quick mind and his brilliance and his ability to help people heal when sick, to turn lights on and off with his mind, to speed up and slow down time, and to manipulate reality and make it conform to his wishes. I really should have realized that I, too, was being made to conform–to his wants and needs, to create a comfortable home for him, not to leave. With me he was able to be more financially stable than he'd ever been in the past. I, on the other hand, had never been so broke while I struggled to support two people, not just myself. My savings disappeared, as did trips, buying clothes, and other luxuries.

The good news, the way that Spirit was able to use my foolishness and terrible choices for good in spite of me, is that I cleared an enormous amount of karma in the short years Pete and I were together. Hardship, and our marriage was definitely hard sailing, when consciously accepted and worked with, can lead to the releasing of a great deal of karma.

It was a turbulent voyage, often fraught with high

seas, and at times I felt drunk, my mind muddled, my ability to see the horizon clouded, unable to steer my own course, but I never abandoned ship. I probably should have, but I didn't.

We had a small, simple wedding. Alice, my friend and witness turned to me just before I went to sign the marriage certificate and joked, "You only get married once the first time." I looked at her, completely startled. She liked Pete–lots of people did; he was a charmer. Alice, not given to prescience, must have felt it too, though. She sent me off to my marriage with a reminder that this was only the first one, the first stop on a longer voyage–a smiling messenger recalling agreements I'd never known I'd made, of promises made by me, perhaps, and by my unseen helpers as well.

I'd never told her about the warning I'd received that my first husband would die. I hadn't even told Pete. He had received his own warnings of an early death, periodically and with clarity, as he grew up.

On some level Alice knew that this choice to marry Pete, however foolhardy, would turn out okay for me in the end. She smiled, laughed, and said, "Come on." You need those friends, the optimistic, cheery ones, to help you take bold, courageous steps, to steer you as you travel into deep and uncharted waters.

Shipwreck

A couple of years later we ran into a friend of Pete's at the store who looked at him and joked, "You're still alive? You're not dead yet?" Another friend called and left a message on the machine, kidding, asking whether Pete had died and that was why he hadn't returned his call. People commented to him that he should lose weight and that he didn't look well. Pete told me that he had been to the doctor and that everything was fine, but later I discovered that he hadn't been to see the doctor at all, that in fact he hated and feared doctors and hadn't been to one since he was a child.

I got a lousy flu that lasted for almost a week. Several friends had that seasonal misery, and it laid one out flat. A week after I had recovered, Pete was home in bed with what I assumed was his turn at the flu. I was supposed to visit my mother, but I phoned her in the morning to say that I would arrive later in the day because Pete wasn't feeling well and I was going to take care of him before leaving.

He was angry with me. "Go," he insisted. "Go. Just go, I'm fine. I'll be fine. Go see your mother. Don't worry about me. Leave." He was emphatic. It wasn't like him to speak to me like that. "I went to the doctor again yesterday," he insisted. "I've just got the same flu that everyone's had, the flu that's going around. That's all. I'll be fine. Go see your mother." Later I wondered if he had a date planned and needed me out of the way. In retrospect, it seems likely.

I ignored his order for me to leave him and went to bring him something to drink instead. I wonder now what it would have been like if I had left as he had directed me. I think I would have felt even worse if I'd returned a couple of days later and found him lying there dead, perhaps in bed, perhaps at the computer, perhaps just on the floor. For me, I think that it would have been much worse. I think that I would have felt guilty despite the fact that he had absolutely insisted that I leave him alone, leave the state, even. I think that it might have taken me a lot longer to overcome the pain and the "what ifs."

Pete continued to refuse to go to the doctor. He refused to go to the hospital. "Let's just go see a doctor," I said.

"No. I'm fine. I told you, I'm fine. I've already been. It's nothing. Leave me alone!" Pete was not one you could make do anything. Stubborn. Obstinate. An immovable force.

If he hadn't lied about having been to the doctor then, and at other times, we would have discovered his diabetes and would have known about his other health issues as well. Instead, I found out from his mother after he died that Pete would have only pretended to go to the doctor and that he hadn't been to see one in at least a couple of decades.

Meanwhile, Pete didn't seem to be feeling much better, so I called my mother again around noon to say that I would come to see her the next day. "Go." He seemed to be pushing me, begging me. He wanted me to leave. He really wanted me out of the house. For better or for worse, I was just as determined to stay. I got him an early dinner, his favorite sandwich at the local sandwich shop–a travesty to my Jewish ancestry: roast beef and cheese. He ate most of it and seemed to enjoy it. We took a nap. I slept on the day that he died. Shouldn't we have been talking? Shouldn't we have been telling each other deep and important truths with our final bits of time together?

"It looks like you're feeling better," I said.

"I am," he told me, getting up and appearing energized.

"Can I get you anything else," I asked him after he returned to bed.

"Yeah," he replied, "ten million bucks." We both laughed. Now, of course, having been with other people toward the end of their lives, I know that it is fairly common for someone who is nearing his time to perk up. I've even heard of cases when people who have been silent or confused for days suddenly speak clearly to those gathered. I know this now, but I didn't then.

Pete laughed some more and then stopped abruptly. He turned away from me and looked toward the end of the bed. He was looking at something, but I saw nothing.

"No! No, not yet. It's too soon," he exclaimed, waving his arms in front of him to emphasize the point.

"What's going on here?" I thought. I looked where he was looking, but I couldn't see anything. His behavior was weird, even for him. There was a different feeling in the room, though, a sort of presence. Pete seemed to be listening to something he was being told.

"I'm not ready," he insisted. "It's too soon." Again his arms were protesting toward where he was looking.

Again he seemed to listen. "No, not yet," he said a final time. He seemed distressed, and I didn't know what to do. I had never seen anything like this before. Clearly he was speaking with someone. In fact, it felt like three someones to me, although I have no idea why. Pete stopped and nodded his head. He seemed to understand something. He seemed calm. And then with a very focused, intense look in his eyes he turned toward me and said, "Kiss me." I kissed him as he continued to stare intently at me. "Please leave the room for a moment," he told me. He was alert, focused, and a bit annoyed.

"Leave me alone for a minute. I want some time to myself."

"No," I said. This was really too strange, and I wasn't about to leave him right then.

He glanced away from me and then turned back to me and said, "Please leave the room for a moment. Everything's fine. Everything's okay. I just need a minute to myself." He seemed so clear, so definite. I felt as if I couldn't say "no" and couldn't see the harm in it anyway. I walked out of the room.

After I left it felt as if a thousand invisible hands were holding me all around. I felt enveloped in love and gentleness. It was such a sweet and comforting feeling, and I closed my eyes to relax into the enfolding calm. After a bit I tried to walk back towards the bedroom. The unseen force that had surrounded me seemed to resist, inhibiting my return to Pete. Surely I could have forced my way, but I just let myself be held a little longer. I don't really remember this time clearly. It wasn't long. Suddenly I felt the hands release me. I called to Pete. He didn't answer. I called out again, suddenly panicked.

I entered the room and saw him lying there, eyes open yet without recognition. His mouth was open too, but he wasn't breathing. He was dead. He was very clearly dead. I felt overwhelmed with nausea and horror. A sense of revulsion, of a tremendous "No!" rushed over me. I thought I would vomit. I thought I might faint. I tried to do CPR, but without success.

Neighbors with medical skills came, and emergency workers arrived quickly and went through the motions of trying to help him. When I think back on the expressions on their faces, I know that they realized that Pete was dead the moment they saw him, just as I had.

Meanwhile, I was packing to go to the hospital. Somehow I had decided that Pete would have one of those miraculous recoveries you read about. I looked at Pete lying there with the emergency worker sitting next to him, writing something down. Then I looked up to the right and couldn't believe what I saw. Pete was standing right there in front of me, looking at me and appearing quite solid. "Do something!" he said.

I looked around the room frantically as if I could find some way to help him or discover something to do for him, something perhaps that the paramedics had overlooked. My neighbor and friend came over to me to tell me that Pete was dead. I think that the paramedics were waiting for me to realize it on my own; they certainly weren't trying to revive him. I was angry. Why weren't they trying to save him?

My neighbor hugged me. I cried on his shoulder, grateful that he was there to tell me the obvious in a gentle way that I could hear. I looked at my husband, to whom I'd been married for such a short time, once more before being sent downstairs by the paramedics. There was a tremendous hush in the room. Amidst the apparent chaos was complete calm. I felt strangely peaceful. I have never had that exact feeling before or since. There was such quiet and peacefulness, such stillness all around. I really can't describe it. I was startled by the words that flooded my mind. "Appreciate life more, not less," I heard. Those words repeated over and over again in my mind. "Appreciate life more, not less." I was to hear those words many more times over the next few days. I still hear them from time to time, when I forget.

A Girl in Every Port

We were packing up the things in the house. A couple of friends had come over to help out, and we were talking and working. One friend was in the kitchen, wrapping the dishes in sheets of newspaper. I saw a mug that had been given to me by another friend years before. It said, "Viva Nicaragua" on the side and was a striking black and red. "Give it to him," I suddenly heard. I looked at the friend who was packing and realized that he would probably like to have this mug, but another friend had given it to me years before, and I had given up so much lately. I didn't say anything. I walked into the dining room and was boxing up some other things when suddenly I heard a crash. I knew what I would see. I walked into the kitchen and saw the mug broken on the floor. The mug had dropped while he was trying to pack it. He was very sorry. I knew that he was, and I wasn't mad. Not at him. I felt angry with myself that I hadn't listened to the guidance I'd received and just given him the mug. It was a small thing, and it was apparently meant to be his at that juncture in our lives. I had given him other possessions that had belonged to Pete and some things that were mine as well–so strange that I tried to hold onto that small object despite the clear prompting to let it go. This was a time of letting go, of releasing the illusion of control over life, of letting go of people, and relationships, and things, and I wasn't learning the lesson deeply enough that we are only given our gifts to hold onto for a while. We're supposed to have things and share things and pass them on as guided. As my mother-in-law likes to say, "I've never seen a hearse pulling a U-Haul truck." If we are open, the time for letting go is quite clear.

A couple of days after the mug shattered, I had an appointment downtown to get an AIDS test. In my heart I knew that I did not have AIDS, but I had just found out that my late husband had been cheating on me. I didn't know how many different people he had slept with during our time together, but it seemed like the number might actually have been quite high. My joke was that he was cheating on the people he was cheating on me with. Gallows humor, I suppose.

One of his paramours got upset when she found out about another lover, starting to raise her voice with me on the phone, "What do you mean that he was going out with Bethany? He couldn't have been seeing Bethany."

"Yeah. He was. The facts are clear."

"But he said he wasn't going out with anyone else."

"You do realize that he wasn't supposed to be going out with you either, right? He was married to me and wasn't supposed to have anyone on the side, let alone several people."

"Several! How could he do that to me? No, that's impossible."

"Stop talking now."

"But he said that he loved me and…"

"Shut up. It's time for you to stop talking."

Crying, "But that can't be true… He said…"

"I'm hanging up the phone now. Don't call me

again."

Another of Pete's girlfriends called three times before I finally got it through her head that I never wanted to speak with her again. She was upset when she found out that he had died and kept wanting more details and information and, unbelievably, to "process" the events with me. Narcissism can lead to so many forms of blindness. And callousness. She kept calling the widow because she was upset that her boyfriend, my late husband, had died.

It took some effort on my part before she understood that I really had no interest in speaking with her again. After a while I wasn't really even upset anymore at the cheating. Disgusted with Pete, yes. I was amazed at the sad and lost and lonely people he had found to comfort and attach to him while he was alive. I was in disbelief that he seemed to have spent much of his waking hours not earning a living or cooking or cleaning up the house or doing anything else useful that would have contributed to the better functioning of our home, our marriage, and our finances during the long hours while I was at work. Instead, he was constantly chasing women. Somehow I still grieved his death and the loss of the man I had believed to be my friend and partner, but I was utterly repulsed by the mountain of lies I had encountered, by his lack of honor and decency, and by his selfishness.

So many, many lies. So much deception. "Rudderless" was the word that came to me periodically. Without following a larger and greater Being, a wiser and deeper Truth to lead us through life, we were truly lost. Whether wandering in a desert or through the wilderness of our egos in mental confusion and emotional self-absorption, if we didn't have a guiding Light we were going to be hopelessly lost as we tried to chart a course through life, its challenges, lessons, and hurdles–on our own.

I figured out who a few of his girlfriends were, but I had no idea of the rest. I didn't need to know who they were. Their identities no longer mattered to me at all. Just people. Just people Pete went out with to try to get attention, to feel special, to have excitement and distraction, and to try to like himself more, even if it were only for an hour or two at a time. That was his story, and I just didn't have the energy to get very interested in it, but I needed to protect myself. First I had gone to a gynecologist and been tested for the possibility of other diseases. Yuk. Now it was time for the AIDS test.

The man who drew my blood was kind. He listened to my story. He seemed to be gay. I wondered whether he himself had the disease. I wasn't concerned that I might somehow get it from him. I knew better than that, but as I looked at him I wondered what he had been through, about how many people he had loved and then lost, both friends and lovers, about the depth of the suffering and the betrayals he'd heard about, and about the times when people had unwittingly given someone else the disease; AIDS was tantamount to a death sentence at that time. Surely he had also witnessed instances when people had knowingly subjected others to AIDS.

My story felt small and my loss rather ordinary. I wondered how he told people the news if it turned out that they were sick; I imagined that he was very good at it, coming from the compassion and wisdom he had gained in the face of so much suffering. How many people had he had to tell that they had the disease? Would he eventually succumb to it himself? I could feel that he did not believe that I had AIDS. How is it that we communicate with each other in this way? Despite my fear, how did I know deep down that I was fine? How did he know? We knew, but we also knew that it was important for me, for everyone, to get tested anyway. It was about taking care of oneself and also making sure that, eventually, when there was someone else in my life, that person would be safe as well.

It took a week for the results to come back, and, as expected, they were clear; I did not have AIDS. Of course, Pete had only died the month before at that point, so if he had been infected at the very end of his life, it might not have shown up in me yet. I would need to get another test later, after more time had passed. I felt relieved, though, and later when I went for another test I heard what I had intuitively known: I was fine.

Mal de Mer

A few days later I was getting ready in the morning, about to head downtown for an appointment. Suddenly I heard, "Put a Band-Aid in your purse."

I thought, "Why do I need Band-Aids? No need."

Again I was told to put a Band-Aid in my purse. I didn't want to. I didn't want to listen to this trivial intrusion. How could it possibly matter whether or not I had a Band-Aid in my purse? Anyway, what was this voice that kept telling me what to do?

I almost walked out of the house without following the directive and then decided that it really couldn't hurt anything to follow this request, so I went upstairs to the bathroom, grabbed a few Band-Aids, and stuck them in my purse. This will not save anyone's life, I thought. How could this possibly be important?

Reluctance and resistance were two of the most recurrent themes in my life. Those, and clinging to the idea that I had a measure of control over my life.

After my appointment I went to a coffee place nearby. The shop was warm and cozy, and I looked forward to sitting for a long time and relaxing, reading the book I had brought while I sipped from my cup. I'd been through an emotional roller coaster and was spending my time packing and donating and dealing with all of the turmoil and busyness that comes with the end of a lifetime. I was looking forward to taking a break and having some down time.

I went to the counter to order tea and a pastry. The woman standing behind the display case of goodies was extremely unpleasant. I no longer remember the things that she said or how she said them. I do remember that she appeared to be angry and unhappy and was giving out a lot of dirty looks. I remember that she made some unpleasant remarks to me and that I had more than one opportunity to respond in a similar way, to point her rudeness out to her and to the others in line, but I didn't. I could have embarrassed her in front of the other customers, belittling her for what they had surely also noticed–she was going out of her way to be nasty to people, unprovoked in any way. I could have "put her in her place," but instead I just thanked her for my things and ignored all that she said.

I found an open spot and sat down to read. Sometimes I would look up from my book and notice that the young woman behind the counter wasn't being very nice to yet another customer. I let it go. My husband had just died, and I was sad and grieving for him and grieving for the loss of what I had thought my life was and would be. I was feeling sorry for myself. I was still numb from all of the lies that had been uncovered after he died. I was busy with mourning and self-pity; her problems just didn't concern me.

After a while I went back to the counter to get some more hot water for my tea. She was rude again. I let it go. Pete had often said that life was too short for fighting. Usually this was in the context of not wanting to fight with me. Not wanting to fight made sense. His not wanting to be a better husband or a better person never did make much sense to me. He hadn't wanted to argue because he hadn't wanted to face the fact that once again he wasn't working and wasn't looking for a job, that he spent too much money, and that he never helped out in the house with cooking or cleaning even though he didn't work much and I was working constantly. He didn't want to fight about it–life was too short. He didn't want to change or contribute, either, but he was right about the not fighting bit.

I've always heard that both people are part of the problem when there are difficulties in a marriage. What I learned over the years is that while it takes two people to have a good marriage–two mature, healthy, and contributing adults–it only takes one person to ruin a marriage.

As I discovered after his passing, he had been a worse husband than I had realized, but I had learned a lot through being married to him, and this was one of his lessons for me. There's too much complaining and fussing and arguing in the world. This is not what life is about. This is not what life is for. This is not how we will want to remember each other. Life is short. I let it go.

I read my book. I drank my tea. For a couple of hours I lost myself in the warmth of the café and my book and the quiet I felt within.

Suddenly I heard screaming. "I cut myself. I cut myself." The woman behind the counter had cut her hand while slicing a bagel for a customer. She looked scared and very upset. "Does anyone have a Band-Aid?" She seemed quite frantic.

"How bad could it possibly be?" I thought.

"Does anyone have a Band-Aid?" No one responded to her. They just looked at her, the rude lady who dispensed drama with each cuppa. Then I remember the Band-Aids I'd tucked into one of the pockets of my purse before I'd left the house that morning.

"I do," I said. I went over to the counter and gave them all to her. She looked at me with sudden recognition. Did she remember being mean to me? She was relieved and grateful, thanking me repeatedly. "No problem," I assured her. "No problem."

Whale Watching

I smiled at the woman behind the counter. I understood why I had been asked to bring the Band-Aids, but the command still didn't fully make sense. I returned to my seat. I was glad that I was able to help, but really, the young woman was just fine. I had seen her hand, and while the cut might have smarted and was bleeding, it didn't look bad. She'd been really upset, but now she was calm. A small gesture created a meaningful result.

Yet why did my guides instruct me to bring Band-Aids that morning? They had been insistent. It couldn't just be about the cut on her hand. Her hand would be just fine. I had not healed her in any physical way at all. This lesson was not about the physical. The cut was pretty minor. Band-Aids, almost by definition, were superficial and often not even necessary. But they made a big difference to her. Maybe she felt taken care of or that people were interested in her in ways that went beyond her ability to dispense coffee and snacks.

I realized that in that moment I was able to forgive her for her previous behavior. I suppose that is why I couldn't remember later any of what it was that she had said. Her comments no longer mattered at all. Why hold onto the words when they were insignificant? This story was not about how she had wounded me with sharp remarks. This story wasn't the tale of how I didn't lash out in return. I'm glad that I didn't respond unkindly, but my guides probably knew that I wouldn't be rude to her just as they'd known that she would cut herself; learning how to speak with people who are rude wasn't my central lesson on that particular day.

It was interesting to me how such a small gesture helped this woman feel cared about and safe. It was clear that a smile and a simple gesture had healed and forgiven the past, the unspoken rift between us. Would I remember this in the future when someone called out to me for some assistance? What other little gifts had I been asked for lately that I hadn't offered?

I hadn't given a friend a mug and moments later it had fallen to the floor. Again, I don't really think that the suggestion was about the mug, although it would have made a nice little gift. It was about the gesture of the mug. It was about the giving itself. Knowing that I had enough despite being broke, knowing that I could listen to the guidance and be led toward a greater gentleness, more kindness, and more peace, were some of the lessons that characterized this time in my life. I was being asked to share. I was being asked, for the thousandth time, to simply follow. I was being taught forgiveness, in small things, so that I could develop my forgiveness muscle, eventually forgiving bigger things such as Pete's many deceptions.

The objects were tiny: a few Band-Aids, an old mug. These items really had no monetary value at all. I kept looking for the message, the meaning on the physical level, but that was not the level on which the lesson was being offered. The message was not about the thing. The message was about reaching out to another person and extending compassion and a generosity of spirit. The friend helping me pack after Pete's death had loved him and thought of him as an elder brother. I knew how much Pete had helped him during his life. This young man spoke of

Pete having been his first real friend. He had lived with us for a time when he had had nowhere else to go. I had told him to pick out some things that had belonged to Pete that he would like to keep. I don't remember what he selected, but perhaps he also needed something from the kitchen to recall meals eaten together. I'm sad that I didn't offer the mug to him. He never asked for anything; he was only there helping out, yet I had heard the request and had ignored it. I'm sorry, friend. It wasn't about the mug. It was about my willingness to give of myself and to respond to another's unspoken need.

When I returned to teaching, I kept Band-Aids on hand for the students. I have given out Band-Aids for the tiniest cuts imaginable. I kept them in a cupboard, so each student had to come up to me and ask specifically for a Band-Aid. I hope that they remember the subjects that I tried to teach them, but maybe my teaching and their learning and my learning wasn't only about the subject matter. Or the homework. Or the rules. It was about learning how to take care of each other. It was about gifts, about delving deeper into the box that Pandora opened, looking under the misery, pain, and suffering on offer to discover subtler, richer blessings. Maybe the ancient Greek tellers of Pandora's tale didn't realize that past the anger there was forgiveness waiting to be unwrapped, hidden behind the fear was courage, and underneath the grief was compassion.

Yet the question remains about how this whole thing works. What is going on when I suddenly hear that I am to do something? At the time of the request, the reasons for giving mugs or Band-Aids are usually not yet apparent. Sometimes a few minutes, hours, or days need to pass before I can see why I needed to listen to that advice. It might take weeks, or in the case of the message about the death of my first husband, it would take years before I would understand what was said. There are things I've done because I was told to do them for which I am still waiting for an explanation decades later.

Whether I ever figure out the meaning behind all of the directives I've been given over the years or not, I've been taught to take these messages of faith, on faith. I've been instructed to do something without having any idea what it could be for, why it is needed, or perhaps how it could possibly make any difference at all. Maybe I will eventually see the results and purpose of all of the actions taken, but then would they still be lessons in faith?

Sometimes, like in the case of rushing to Berlin, I've examined the time I spent there and the urgency of the directive to get there, and I still don't think I truly understand that experience or why I was sent. I have moved through most of my life without understanding what was taking place or what meaning a moment held. Circumstances, guidance, and assistance passed by, often, unrecognized and unpraised. God was fully present, but frequently I failed to notice.

How does it work that Spirit knows that a woman I will be around later that day will want Band-Aids, not have any herself, that no one else in the whole café will have any, and so I need to bring some? How does Spirit know who will be at the café, what they will have in their purses, or that she will cut herself? Are all of these things seen as facts in advance? As probabilities?

The young woman likely thought that cutting herself had been an accident. What if the slip of the knife wasn't a sudden act at all, but planned or orchestrated? Maybe her cutting herself in that moment, having that job even, in that city, at that time, had all been decided far in advance. Maybe everyone who was scheduled to be there had shown up for his or her appointments. Perhaps women who had walked by the coffee shop, their purses crammed with Band-Aids for their children and strangers alike, had decided to take their morning coffee elsewhere to allow for the perfect unfolding of events, for them to be at their own rendezvous with fate and teachings and faith.

Safe Harbor

After Pete died I moved back home. My old bedroom was rented out, so I moved into the smaller guest room and set about getting my life and mind and finances back in order.

I got a job in the service sector because teaching required more emotional equilibrium and stamina than I had at that time, and I focused on paying off all of the bills that Pete had hidden from me. It was a bleak time. I read *A Course In Miracles*, prayed a lot, worked a lot, didn't spend any money, went for walks with friends, and paid off the bills one by one.

I cooked meals, ran errands, and helped out around the house in order to pay a bit of "rent." One day my mom, who didn't like to drive at night by this time, had an appointment in another city. I was off that day and offered to drive her there and back, deciding to take a rare bit of downtime in the beautiful gardens located not far from her meeting. I dropped her off, arranged for when I'd be back to pick her up, and then I found the city park, walked over to a green and silent spot, and sat down on a bench.

As I became quieter, turbulent emotions that I had been stuffing away just to keep going while getting my life back on track began to surface. I started to cry, gazing at the flowers and trees while praying and feeling a deep sadness. Suddenly I became aware of the plants and trees near me in a different way. They were leaning closer, some of their leaves now touching my shoulders and head, and they were sending me comfort and peace.

Plant wisdom is different than people wisdom. Plants understand cycles of growth and the losing of leaves, fallow times, death, and regeneration. They understand that all of life is connected, that while life may die out in one place, it will sprout somewhere else, perhaps carrying a different form. People breathe out and plants breathe in the carbon dioxide expelled by human beings and then return the favor by exhaling oxygen for the oxygen-dependent humans in their midst. Plants feel the seasons shift, the winds move, and the earth's silent breath.

I can't prove that the plants leaned in to comfort me that day, although I've read amazing studies about plant consciousness and I've seen and felt understanding in and through them–I can't prove it, but for me it was real. I let go of a piece of grief I had been carrying with me that day and was filled with a sense of communion with life, with its goodness, and with the eternity that is our true home.

Fathoms Deep

Eventually, although I still had plenty of bills left to pay, I had enough money that I was able to go on vacation for a few days in the cooler northern climes, staying cheaply in a dorm room with some other women–it reminded me of my time in Youth Hostels. I was, after all, a bit of an expert in bargain travel.

It was summer, the weather was perfect for swimming in a nearby lake, and I met people who, perhaps through an inadvertent remark on my part to someone, realized that I had intuitive abilities. After that, everyone I met wanted a reading.

"Sure," I told them, and over my few days there I gave free readings to several different people. No names or other identifying information will be given here because the world is a small place, but of the three sessions I'm going to describe, all details presented are accurate to the best of my recollection.

The first woman told me nothing about herself, an African American woman a bit older than myself, her husband sitting quietly nearby. I didn't know what to expect–I never know what information will come through, or how, or whether it will be clear and detailed or rather vague, if it will be easy to obtain, or a struggle to access. With every reading I give I feel like I'm diving into deep and uncharted waters. It's an act of trust, of faith, that something will meet me in these unknowable, fathomless depths and will give me images or information that I can understand and pass on to the person waiting expectantly in front of me. It's gotten a little bit less scary over the years.

"Your grandmother is here. She had southern roots, lots of pain and struggle in her ancestry. She was a strong, powerful woman. She says that you're named for her." My client looks me in the eye at that remark and nods, casting a brief sideways glance at her husband. I'm getting that she's attached to you through your spleen. She loved you deeply, but fiercely. She still hasn't let you go. She doesn't really like me telling you all of this. I'm not exactly sure where the spleen is and I don't know what it does, but she died because of something to do with her spleen.

"That's true," the lady told me. "She was fierce and demanding, but I always knew she loved me. And she did die because of her spleen. A couple of years ago."

"Well, I'm getting that you haven't been fully well since that time. I'm getting that you're now having trouble with your spleen as well. I feel like your grandmother is trying to pull you over to the other side to be with her. It seems like she's connecting to you through your spleen."

"Yes, I've been sick too. I haven't been really well since she died, but the doctors haven't found anything specific. My grandmother comes to mind all of the time. I don't have peace around her death, but we didn't always get along."

"Well, I'm telling her to leave you alone. You need to tell her to leave you alone as well. You have a life of your own to live. She needs to make peace with herself and her lifetime and move on. Let's thank her for her love and support and for every time she was kind and helpful, forgiving her for everything else as best we can. Let's send her on her way with gratitude and blessings."

The reading ended after some more discussion, and she thanked me profusely.

A couple of days later I saw the lady and her husband again.

"I've changed my name," she told me, telling me of the African name that she'd always loved that she'd selected for herself.

I tuned into her energy. "Your grandmother's gone," I said. "She's in the Light now. You're safe; you sent her on. Changing your name was a great idea. She can still visit you from time to time, but from now on she'll check in on you without draining your health and vitality; she also has her own work to do since she's in the Light, so she's busy. Your grandmother can hear you as well, so talk to her whenever you like and trust that she heard you."

"I know. I can still feel her, but I feel peaceful about her death now, like it was her time to go and that it's all okay. I feel so much better and clearer. I feel free and like I'm going to be fine now. Thank you so much."

"Of course. What a relief. I'm so glad it worked out."

It's decades later now, and although that situation had a powerful healing and positive outcome, today, I would do things differently. Over the years I've had much more experience and developed a greater understanding of "spirit attachments," those people who have passed but are hanging around and haven't yet crossed into the Light.

Today, when I work with someone who has a spirit attachment in their energy field, whether they're around them all of the time or just visit them periodically, I send away that departed soul, firmly, using a number of techniques I've developed over the years. The deceased person is directed into the Light right then and there. The spirit is not allowed to hang out as a ghost.

I did tell the spirit to leave her granddaughter alone, but Grandma didn't want to leave behind her human life, personal connections, and earthly attachments. Now I have methods I've developed that detach spirits from the people they're following around. I usually get immediate results, although sometimes it can take as long as a couple of days. Eventually, though, I get the spirit to release the lifetime that has ended and to head into the Light. I didn't know how to do that very back then, and each experience is different. The process is a dialogue, and the shifting of energy occurs with the help of angelic forces beyond my ability to explain or describe clearly. The granddaughter, however, found her own solution to the problem, and it worked perfectly.

Abandon Ship

I have come to believe that when we die it is our job to head straight into the Light. Some traditions believe that after death the soul stays with people, loved ones, and its home and earthly experiences for a while, whether that be for three days or forty days or whatever. I'm not a huge fan of this idea. Waving good-bye as one immediately heads to the brilliant and all-encompassing, perfect white Light protects both the departing soul and the friends and loved ones left behind. In the Light one completes a life review and then can send love to and can communicate, safely, with those still completing lifetimes on Earth.

I have encountered souls who are occupying the energy fields of people I meet, usually without them being aware of this fact, and almost always without their permission or agreement of any kind (never give another human being permission to share your energy field–that's co-dependence of an extreme variety), and these souls might have been there for months, for years, for decades, or even hanging around a family or place for generations. Most people don't quite have enough energy with which to live their own lives, never mind having sufficient energy to lug one or more departed "people" around with them, ghosts that are siphoning off the energy reserves of the "host." Usually, these ghosts just make the person they're hanging onto more tired or confused, but sometimes the results can lead to mental and other forms of illness, to depression and anxiety, and to utter exhaustion.

Over the years I've had extended arguments with spirits who wanted to continue to occupy a home, hotel, person or persons, or other locations. "But I'm really nice," one deceased woman told me. "I don't cause problems for anyone. It's not an issue. I just like it here. I don't need to leave. I'm good, not evil."

I agreed that she had probably been a nice person but insisted that she needed to head to the Light anyway. The Light is our natural home. It doesn't matter whether one was a kind person or not. Even if people caused great harm to others while on earth, the Light will still welcome their return. Regardless of the manner in which one died, including due to suicide, and no matter what one's religious beliefs are or are not, everyone is meant to return to God's embrace. We all come from God, from the Light, and we're all eternal beings made of light. It is our job, when our lifetime on earth has ended, to return home.

An important note needs to be mentioned here. Very rarely I have encountered people who, after they passed away, got confused and got it wrong. In two cases I encountered, highly religious, conservative Christians who believed in a God who judged them heavily and who might want to punish them for eternity, both made a wrong turn. These good people were tricked by what I believe was the Antichrist, a truly frightening being I didn't even believe in until, to my horror, I encountered it as it tried to hold these people prisoner in what I can only describe as a sort of hell. It took a fair amount of work, but I got each of them out of there. In one case it took me almost three months. The other situation was resolved more quickly, but both instances were scary to me, and the entire process felt threatening. I worked carefully, slowly, and under the direct guidance of my protective angels.

Those people now reside in the perfect white Light

where they belong.

What are we supposed to do when we die? We head to the Light. I believe that people should be careful, regardless of religious orientation, and that everyone has the same final destination. We head to the most brilliant white Light we could ever imagine. Some people see bits of gold or silver in this white Light, but that's it. An astonishingly brilliant white Light, perhaps with hints of silver and/or gold as well, is the final port of call. Under no circumstances head toward a light that is white with bits of pink, red, or orange in it. That is not good, safe, or healing. That is hell.

Barnacles On the Hull

Another woman I worked with that summer was someone staying in a nearby hotel. Word that I was giving out free readings must have traveled about quickly. As we sat down to work together, this woman, a rather pale, wan, and tired-looking lady, told me her first name, let's call her Penny, and that she wanted to contact her sister who had died the year before. Could I do that?

She was grieving and couldn't process or release some of the pain she was feeling, which was why she looked so depleted and fatigued. Since her deceased sister was already sitting with us, I assured her that we could talk to her right now.

"Penny, your sister is saying that you shouldn't do what she did. She's saying that you need to change your life and do things differently. She doesn't want you to make the same mistakes she made," I explained.

"That's too vague. That is something you could say to anyone. What else is she saying?"

I had to agree that those words sounded quite general, but the sister kept repeating the same message over and over again, only varying her words slightly, so maybe although on the surface those words sounded general, my guess was that they meant something specific and that my "client" knew exactly what I was talking about.

"Your sister won't let this go. You're making the same mistakes she did. She's trying to warn you. She says that you're not listening to her now, just like she didn't listen to people who were trying to help her while she was alive."

"That's too general. You could be talking to anyone about anything," Penny responded a bit aggressively. Clearly I wasn't telling her what she wanted to hear, which often happens in life, whether we're speaking to the dead or not.

"Could it be that you don't like what your sister is telling you and that you understand what she's saying, but that you just don't like it?" I replied.

"No. That's too general. It could mean anything."

After the third repetition, the woman receiving my time and energy for free was getting even more fed up with me. It's funny, sometimes, how demanding people can be. They want what they want, and they want it how they want it! It doesn't matter if we're strangers. It doesn't matter if I'm doing this as a gift. I knew this pattern. I'd been guilty of it myself. A loving angel would give me clear guidance for something I was supposed to do or change in my life, and I'd proceed to argue with it. The advice wasn't convenient or it didn't make sense to my logical mind or it would require me to really grow or it dictated big changes in my life. Whether the advice given from wiser, loving beings suggested small changes, little corrections in my course, or giant ones, I often didn't want to do what I was being told. I could be really pig-headed too. No doubt about it!

Unhealed pain can make people unkind, and as I was about to discover, the sister's death was only a recent example of pain experienced in a life in which pain began early.

"Ask her how she died," the lady asked. "That's what I want to know about."

I turned within my mind back to the sister waiting with us and asked her to tell me how she'd passed away.

"She says that she doesn't want to talk about it. She says that you already know how she died. She wants you to listen to her. You're making the same mistakes she did."

"Ask her how she died," my client demanded again.

"She keeps telling me that you know perfectly well how she died."

"I don't care about that! Ask her how she died!"

"She really doesn't want to talk about it. It's painful to her. Anyway, you already know this." Clearly we weren't dealing with some sort of mysterious event here. The facts were known. I got that the deceased was in the Light, but she still hadn't been able to fully clear or process what had happened to her in the lifetime she had so recently left.

"Make her tell you how she died!"

In my mind I began to speak with the sister: "Penny needs you to tell me about how you died. I'm sorry. I know you don't want to do it, but I don't think that she can believe that I'm really speaking with you unless you tell me about it."

Images of the sister being stabbed in the neck, shoulders, and upper back began to flood my mind. There was a child nearby. She was in a car. It was her boyfriend who killed her.

"She was stabbed to death by her boyfriend. She says that it was the stab wound to her neck that killed her."

"No, it was the one in the shoulder that killed her."

"No, she says it was the one in the neck that took her out." This woman did not receive information easily. She was not one to lightly change her mind, even in the presence of facts I couldn't possibly have known. The rest of what I was telling her was not being disputed. Why not accept this last little bit of information as true? Another option would have been to dismiss which specific knife wound was the fatal one as insignificant. Her sister was stabbed multiple times in the upper body, in a car, by the boyfriend who didn't care about anything else at that time except making sure that she was good and dead.

If I had been working with Penny, over time we could have addressed her issues around control, the literalness of her thinking, her insistent need to be "right," and so on, but for now I was just trying to help her know that her sister was with her and was fine despite having lived a life that contained a lot of pain and drama.

We spoke for a while. "Your sister is fine now. She's safe. She just doesn't like to think about how she died. It was traumatic, and she knew better. She knew she should never have been with that guy. She lost her life because she didn't listen to her own gut, to what she knew was right for her, and as a result she lost her life, and her child, family, and friends are now suffering. She really regrets the choices she made. And not just with the guy who killed her. With other men she dated as well."

"She's telling me that your father was very abusive, and not just physically. She's saying that you've had abusive relationships as well, and that you're in one right now."

"I'm sorry, but everything that your sister was telling me at the beginning of this session, and that you didn't want to listen to, and that you kept saying was too vague and could mean anything at all, that it was something I could just say to anyone who had lost someone they loved, well, that information doesn't feel vague to me. It feels clear. Your sister is trying to give you a direct warning. Penny, she desperately wants you to hear her. She wants you to listen carefully to her. She wants you to do what you need to do to take care of yourself and to make much better choices. Are you ready to listen now? Do you understand what your sister is saying?"

"Yes. It's true. I know what she's talking about. Our dad was a bastard. I've dated abusive guys too. My current boyfriend is sometimes a jerk. I could die the same way she did."

Soon afterwards I ended the session. Did she go on to change her life, to get rid of the abusive relationships that she had continually experienced? I don't know. I do know that she was hugging me and crying at the end, thanking me over and over again. Clearly, a big shift had occurred.

"You don't know how much this means to me. You don't know how important this is to me. She's okay. That really was her. She's fine. Death isn't the end, and she's okay. She isn't suffering. I feel so much better. I feel so much more at peace. Thank you."

I don't remember which state this woman had travelled from, I couldn't pick her out of a two person lineup, and I certainly don't remember her name, but I remember, quite vividly, the images her sister showed me of her death, and I know that a family received some genuine comfort in the face of their horrible loss.

"Thank you, God," I prayed. "Thank you for teaching me, for using me to help others, for guiding me in my life." At times it was draining, exhausting work. Dangerous at times. Scary at others. Almost always weird. Again and again those experiences demolished all of my previous notions of what was true and what wasn't, of what was possible and what wasn't, about what our lives were for, about what happened when we "die," and on and on. Each time I thought I knew what was true, what was real, and what could or couldn't be, those previous "truths" were shaken or dismantled by the angels and guides that were speaking to and through me. It was a gift–a great gift. Granted, this gift didn't feel good at times, but it was one that I could use to help people, to comfort them, and to do my part to heal some of the tremendous suffering in the world.

Scurvy

The third story from this time in my life that I want to share in this book was for a young woman who radiated good health. For whatever reason, I asked her to lie down because I wanted to do a quick scan over her body. She lay down on the grass where we were sitting and I moved my hands down her body, starting just over her head. I kept my hands about two feet over her, never touching her. My hands seemed to move of their own accord, rushing down from her head to her legs, where they suddenly stopped. I tried the same thing again, positioning my hands above her head and then finding myself pulled strongly down to the area above her legs. Clearly she had an issue with her legs. I felt that the energy in her legs was frozen.

"Polio," I heard. "Polio through the generations."

"Forget it," I thought to myself. "I'm not saying that out loud."

"Polio through the generations," echoed in my mind again.

"I'm not saying that," I insisted. "That's ridiculous. No one in this country gets polio any more, especially not upper class athletes in their early 20s. Polio isn't inherited anyway. That's ridiculous."

In response, the words "Polio through the generations," repeated in my head yet again.

The same information kept coming in. It wasn't changing, and it didn't seem to want to stop. Sighing heavily I looked at her and said, "This is going to sound crazy. It's not even possible, as far as I know, but I feel frozen energy in your legs and I keep hearing that you have polio and that you got it 'through the generations.' It's ridiculous, I know."

"No. That's exactly right. I do have polio. The doctors told me that I'd probably lose my ability to walk at some point."

"But you're such an amazing athlete!"

"That's why I exercise so much. I don't know how long I'll be able to use my full body; I want to take advantage of my mobility for as long as I have it, and I want to put off any loss of movement for as long as possible."

"I know that polio used to be common, but people have been vaccinated for it for a long time. Anyway, you get it from contaminated water and stuff; you don't inherit it."

"*I* did. My father is in the Foreign Service. My family was living in _____ (Insert the name of a poor and distant country here. I have completely forgotten which one it was.), and my mother got a polio vaccine to protect her when they moved there. It turns out that she was already pregnant with me, and the polio passed through her system to mine. I've had polio my whole life. It's just been mostly in a sort of remission. I got it through my mother."

"Amazing."

At this point you might be wondering whom this session was for, her or me? Moments like that are quite common. I'm always learning something new when I give a

254

session to someone. More than that, I'm often astounded at the clarity of transmission, of how I couldn't possibly know anything about the information I'm conveying, and of the power and beauty of those who are working through me. It's humbling. I often find it awe-inspiring. Doing this kind of work has grown and deepened my faith in a present and loving God. And then it's deepened it again. And yet again.

What did this woman learn from me? Something, I hope. I told her about a few other things that were coming through for her. Perhaps the session, from the perspective of her growth and healing, was mostly about remembering her connection to the eternal and unseen, to the angels and holiness that walk beside her throughout her life.

Shore Leave

During this time my grandparents were living in their apartment in Florida full-time, having moved there permanently from the far north when the cold had become a threat to their aging bodies. They lived in their one bedroom apartment, now aided by 24-hour help for my grandfather who hadn't spoken or responded in any noticeable way at all for almost three years. He just lay in his twin bed without moving, a few feet away from my grandmother. She would speak to him and kiss him, but he just lay there. The doctors told us that they didn't know why he was still alive.

I knew why he was alive. He was waiting patiently, like the gentleman he was, for my grandmother in the adjoining bed. He waited that way for three years. He was 100 when I started my new teaching job about a year after Pete's death, and Grandma was 93. She was fading a bit but still able to get about and find things to enjoy about her life. Most days she was completely lucid.

I was leaving work on a late afternoon in September. As I walked down the hall toward the parking lot I passed the main office and suddenly thought, "It's Rosh Hashanah; I'd better call Grandma now, before it gets too late. I asked the secretary if I could use her phone to make a long-distance call and told her that I'd reimburse the school. She said sure and helped me place the call. Grandma and I spoke for a few minutes. I wished her happy holidays, and she wished me well in my new job and city. She was tired, so we hung up soon afterwards.

That was the last time I spoke to her. The next day she had a massive stroke and never spoke again. I'm so glad that my angels told me to stop a moment and make that call. At the hospital the doctors recommended that she be put into hospice care for her remaining days. She lived at home, largely unresponsive, refusing food and liquid until she passed away about a week later. It was a Wednesday. I received the call at work as I sat at my desk grading after the end of the school day. I had been expecting the call at any time. I was sad, but I also realized that she had been ready to go. I immediately called my grandparents' apartment and, after talking to the nurse for a few moments, asked her to hold the phone up next to my grandfather's ear. She did because she believed that he could sometimes hear her regardless of what the doctors said.

"Grandpa, it's me," I spoke loudly into the phone. "Grandpa, I love you. I'm calling because Grandma just died. She just passed away, so it's okay for you to go now too. It's time for you to go now, Grandpa. Grandma's okay, and you'll be okay too. You can let yourself die now, too. I love you."

The nurse got on the phone. "He heard you. I could tell. I think he heard what you said."

I needed to leave the next day, right after work. My grandmother would be flown from Florida to her home state to be buried in the Jewish cemetery there, next to their son, Jacob, who had been run off the road by a drunk driver years before.

Meanwhile, my friend went with me to the mall to buy something to wear to the funeral. I usually like to wear jeans and a sweatshirt, so I never have anything decent to wear should circumstances dictate different apparel. Even at work I dress as casually as the job will allow.

I decided to buy a dress, something rather fancy, because Grandma and I had always argued over my clothes. She had hated that I bought most of my things at thrift stores and that I almost never dressed up.

"It's your funeral, Grandma," I thought. "I'll be wearing a dress." My friend asked me why I was spending so much money. "It has to be nice," I told her. I was at Nordstrom's, and a helpful saleslady had figured out what I was looking for and was picking things out for me from all over the store. I waited in the dressing room as she brought in her finds. I picked out a dark, pretty dress that I thought would be perfect and that I was sure Grandma would have approved of. The sales lady and I started to head to the cash register when I told her, "I'd better get one more."

"What do you mean?"

"I need another outfit to wear to another funeral. My grandmother died today, but I think my grandfather is going to go next. Soon. I think he's only been alive these last few years to keep her company. She was afraid of death and didn't want to be left alone, so he's been waiting for her to be ready to go."

The saleslady looked a little surprised, but her professionalism took over and she fell into action immediately. "Do you want another dress?"

"It doesn't have to be a dress, but it has to be dressy."

Within minutes I was standing in the mirror looking at myself in a nice black pantsuit. It looked great, but needed a little altering. "We'll do it for you tonight," the woman informed me. Given the fact that it must have been around eight o'clock already, I was really impressed. "You can pick it up tomorrow when we open."

"I'll be teaching then. Could I come by at lunch to pick it up?"

"We can bring it to you at your school," she told me.

I was ready. I went home to pack the rest of my things. It would be a Jewish funeral, of course, so it had to be performed within two days of my grandmother's passing. I would arrive Thursday night and the funeral would be on Friday. A colleague offered to cover my last class for me, so I was able to leave school early. I called the airline to book my flight. I told the agent that I needed to leave the next day, on Thursday afternoon. She found an outgoing flight for me and then asked when I wanted to return. I thought about it for a moment. I knew that the rest of my family was arriving on Thursday and leaving on Saturday.

"I'd like to return on Sunday evening," I told her. I was staying with my mom at the hotel. I wouldn't have anywhere to stay on Saturday night and didn't really have much money left for a hotel room of my own. Well, it'll work out, I thought. A relative will let me stay overnight if I ask. Even though my parents and brother had each made plans to leave on Saturday, I knew that I needed to stay until Sunday. I didn't think about it too much. I just left it at that.

Calm Seas

I arrived at the hotel on Thursday evening, spent a little time with my family, and then decided to go take a shower since I felt grungy after my trip. While I was in the shower washing my hair I suddenly felt my grandfather's presence with me. "Hi, Grandpa," I said. I just smiled. I couldn't actually see him, but I knew he was there. It was like he was thinking with me, that our minds were connected.

"I'm going now, too," he told me. I felt his love for me and received his blessing. I felt him communicate to me that they had left me some money and that I should take their furniture, if I wanted. I thanked him. We just expressed our love for each other for a moment, and then he had to leave. I got out of the shower, dried off, wrapped a towel around my head, threw on a robe, and was surprised to see some people in the room when I got out.

"I need to tell you, my father just died," my dad told me. "I got off the phone a couple of minutes ago with his nurse."

"I know," I said. "I just talked to him. He stopped by to say good-bye." I felt peaceful, sharing in some of my grandfather's serenity and happiness. My dad and the other family members there looked at me kind of funny, but they were too preoccupied with their own thoughts to say much. However, there wasn't the least bit of doubt in my mind that I'd just spoken with my grandfather.

This was the first visit through the ethers I had ever received from my grandfather even though he'd been in a sort of coma for the past three years. Of course, he'd just passed away, so perhaps this was his first opportunity. Gramps had seemed happy and peaceful. He hadn't seemed scared or disoriented in any way. He was letting me know that he loved me, that he was with Grandma, that they had left a gift for me, and that it was time for him to go.

Even though the medical authorities had assured us that Gramps had no idea what was going on around him during the last years of his life, I know that I had successfully communicated with him when I had called him the day before to let him know that Grandma had died. Now it was his turn, speaking to me as he departed his earthly lifetime, knowing that I would be able to hear him now even though most people, and certainly most scientists, would tell you that those who have passed on are unable to speak, let alone to speak clearly, to those who are still alive and embodied.

My poor dad looked quite crushed. Even though his parents were 93 and 100 years old, the loss was still hard. It was Thursday night now and normally my grandfather would have been buried on Saturday, but Saturday was Yom Kippur. My grandfather's funeral would have to be held on Sunday.

My mother turned to me, almost accusingly. "You knew," she said. "You knew. You always said he was just waiting for her. You knew this would happen, didn't you?" She wasn't mad, just incredulous. It was as if, after all those years of my weirdness, she got it. She didn't try to explain away my knowing as coincidence, a lucky guess, chance, or being flaky. I had predicted plenty of things before, but for whatever reason, this time she was ready to accept the truth of my prediction without protest. But still she was surprised, stunned. "You knew," she kept repeating. "You've been saying this all along. Oh my God. Your flight doesn't leave until Sunday afternoon, does it?"

"Yeah. I arranged to leave on Sunday."

"Oh my God. You knew. You knew that you needed to stay until Sunday."

"Yes. That's also why I bought two different outfits. I bought one outfit for each funeral."

"You did? You brought two things?" Somehow she was managing to become even more shocked. "You really knew. You always said that this would happen."

"Yes. He was waiting for her. She was afraid of being alone. She didn't want to die, and she didn't want him to die first and leave her alone, so he just waited until it was her time."

"Amazing. Yes, that's just what he did. He was such a kind, good man. And he loved her. He decided to wait." We were both moved, not just by their seventy-three years of marriage, but by his compassion, his patience, his loyalty, and their complete devotion to each other. Grandma would have done anything for him, and he for her. We didn't need proof; their mutual devotion was clear, but here was another indication of their commitment to one another. Grandpa put up with three years of lying in bed, being moved and changed and bathed and fed while waiting silently until it was time to go.

"I need to change my ticket and reserve this hotel room for another night. I won't have time to go shopping. I'll just have to wear the same thing twice," my mom said as she looked over at me.

"That's all right, Mom, so will everyone else."

She laughed. "That's right. Everyone from out-of-town will be wearing the same outfit twice. We'll all have to change our flights and our hotel rooms. Everyone except you." She looked at me again for a long moment as if trying to understand. Trying to see what I saw or understand how I did it. I couldn't have told her. "Things" just came to me, and I tried to listen to and respect the messages I received, or at least I often did. Sometimes the messages were loud, clear, and obvious, at other times subtle and more open to doubt or interpretation, but I was learning to be led. I felt as if I lived my life on standby. Increasingly I tried to get out of my own way and listen and follow the guidance I received as much as my developing faith allowed.

"He spoke to me." I said again. "I couldn't really see him. It was more like I could look at him through my mind. He was smiling. He looked almost relieved. He was definitely happy and he was on his way to be with Grandma. He knew that he was about to see Jacob."

Mom was watching me now. I could see that she really wanted to believe me, not so much because I was her daughter, but because it would mean that we really didn't need to be afraid and that death was not the end. We would see those we loved again. Not only that, but we could speak to them now, and they would hear us because they lived on. What waited for us after we passed away was good and loving and happy and peaceful and unending. I was trying to get her to see and feel what I did.

"He just radiated peace and love. I'll miss him, but we don't have the slightest reason to be sad. He's happy and he's fine. He's with people he loves, and we'll see him again. We don't really die, Mom. We just change our form. We live forever."

I don't think that she completely believed me. Part of her was trying to, though. What I was saying was different than what her church had always told her, but then maybe the church doctrine didn't tell the full story. As always, I was glad that I had listened to the guidance I had received. I had a different outfit for each funeral, and Grandma would be pleased that I was well-dressed. My flight was just when I needed it to be on Sunday, and I even had a place to stay! As is often the case with these encounters, I was humbled and filled with gratitude. God's plan was always better than anything I could come up with on my own. Why did I still try to assert control over my life? Why not give everything over and simply follow? I was trying to listen and follow but was still finding it difficult despite the mounting evidence that God's path for me was the happiest one.

In the Doldrums

After he died, I remembered a conversation my grandfather and I had had years before. I was traveling in Europe and was staying in Germany for a couple of days with a wonderful family I had met before heading to Spain to teach English. The family surprised me by insisting that I call my parents in the States while I was staying at their home. At that time, that was an expensive phone call and a really thoughtful offer. On my own I only called my parents briefly about once every two to three weeks, and my parents had no way to contact me since I was continually moving about. Mostly I wrote post cards and letters because that was cheaper. At my host family's encouragement, I called home. My dad answered the phone and told me that my grandparents were still there with them at the house. They had stopped to visit my parents on their way to Florida and, while they were leaving to continue driving south, they were involved in a bad car accident. My grandmother was okay, but my grandfather had banged his head. "He's still confused and shaken up from the accident," my father told me. "He keeps talking about my brother Jacob. He keeps saying that he saw him. The doctor said that he'll be okay, but that he'll need a while longer to get over the accident."

I was put on the phone with my grandfather. We started talking, and I told him how sorry I was that they had had that accident and how relieved I was that they were going to be okay. Not interested in small talk, my grandfather urgently said, "I saw Jacob. I saw Jacob. I saw him, and we talked."

"Grandpa, you couldn't have seen Jacob; Jacob is dead. He's been dead for many years, Grandpa." I am embarrassed to say that I told him this in a talking-to-a-convalescent-who's-not-quite-right-in-the-head sort of voice. I was patronizing.

"I saw him. I know I saw him. We talked. He's fine. We had a good visit."

"Grandpa, that's not possible."

"I saw him. I saw Jacob." He had told the doctor that he had visited with his deceased son, and the idea had been dismissed as a hallucination from being knocked out. Then Gramps told my dad about what he'd experienced, but Dad wasn't accepting of the concept of conversing with the dead either. Now Gramps was telling me about one of the most important experiences of his life, one that was bringing him comfort since he had spoken to my dad's brother, Jacob, for the first time since Jacob had died almost three decades before–and I wasn't any more understanding or supportive than anyone else had been. Rather than truly hearing him out with an open mind, at barely 20 years old I was reluctant and in denial and arguing with this wise and gentle man I loved, one who wasn't given to flights of fancy.

"Grandpa, Jacob is dead. I'm sorry, but he's dead," I told him.

"I saw Jacob. We talked. I talked to Jacob." His voice was almost pleading now.

There I was, the rational, healthy adult patiently explaining to my aged, injured grandfather, over and over again, that you can't talk to the dead.

268

I was mortified as I remembered that conversation from years before as I sat in the hotel room that night, thinking about my grandfather who had died a few hours earlier and my grandmother who had died the previous day. The memory of my conversation with Gramps almost 15 years earlier haunted me despite feeling nothing but peace around my grandfather's crossing.

"I'm sorry, Grandpa," I called out to him now in my mind as I sat on the edge of my hotel room bed. "I'm sorry. You were right! Of course you talked to Jacob. Of course you did. You were badly injured in the accident. You probably had a near-death experience. He came and saw you. You did visit. You did talk. He probably even told you that you had to go back and finish up your lifetime because it wasn't your time yet. Is he the one who said that you had to return to your body? I'm sorry I didn't listen to you. I'm sorry I kept telling you that you were wrong. I didn't know about those things then–I was actively struggling to not know about those kinds of things. I didn't believe in any of it, even in those experiences I'd had myself. I was an adamant atheist. I argued against anything that couldn't be scientifically proven.

I didn't know.

Not only did you visit with Jacob, no one believed you; no one would listen to what you had to say. I know how horrible that feels! I hope that you didn't doubt yourself because of me. I hope that you held onto your memory and what you knew to be true. I love you, Grandpa."

I could feel his love in return and knew that it was all right. He wasn't mad at me, and he didn't feel like I had let him down. I was angry with myself, though. It was ridiculous. Here I was, weirder than he ever managed to be for ten minutes in his entire lifetime, and I hadn't listened to him. I hadn't taken what he had said seriously. I hadn't respected or valued the truth of his words. I had acted toward him exactly the way most people treated me when I tried to tell them about what I saw that was beyond our most obvious senses, outside of visible, logical experience. Other people had often been patronizing toward me as well. They talked down to me as if to some poor, misguided, perhaps mentally unstable, well, let's call it like they saw it, mentally ill, woman who had delusions, heard voices, you name it! I had been on the receiving end of that attitude, and worse, an endless number of times. I still hated it when it happened, but at least now maybe I could understand that attitude toward the unknown. Until these psychic experiences became a part of my daily routine, I had laughed at such ideas too; in fact, I'd made fun of them mercilessly. I had ridiculed the religious and scoffed at the sacred. I had made fun of the intuitive, the mystical, the unproven and unseen. I had been exactly like that.

High and Dry

And then things started to change. I had hated the visions, the voices, the inexplicable knowing of information. I fought hard against all of it for years. Then, little by little, I relented. It was real. I couldn't touch it or spell it or take a picture of it, but it was real. It was real and important. Intuitive abilities were talents to be developed and accessed by everyone, and they held the key to our lives, to our purpose, to why we were here.

I had finally listened and moved west with the contents of my small car, so I owned a limited wardrobe, bedding, towels, and toiletries, some books, and a few things for the kitchen. I slept on the floor on an air mattress. At night I would refill it with air and in the morning I would wake up to discover that my head, shoulders, and rear end were flat against the floor. I would wake up tired and sore, but it took some months to be able to afford a bed. I found a rickety table and two chairs that someone had left out by the dumpster. By putting the table in a corner where it had support from the walls on two sides, and by sitting very gingerly on the chairs, I had a dinette set/work space. I made do, but I was beginning to get tired of my apartment. It was really small and overlooked the parking lot, so there was always noise and too much light. The apartment was also next to the stairwell, and I could hear the hallway doors to the stairway slamming and people charging up and down the steps at all hours, shaking the floor of my room. I wanted to move to a better, more comfortable apartment.

"Why don't you move into the apartment across the hall," I heard. That didn't make any sense to me. I had seen the people who lived across the hall a few times. There was a young mother and her child, plus a guy with a very large snake living there. They were living there and didn't seem to have any intention of moving. This time, I thought, the voice got it wrong.

My grandparents had passed away that September. My father asked me whether I wanted any of their things. "What's going to happen to their furniture?" I asked. "Are you going to take it?"

"No, I was going to sell some and give the rest away. You don't want their stuff. It's old and beat up."

I convinced him that since I didn't have any furniture except for a bed and a bookcase at that point, that I would like it. I remembered my grandfather coming to visit me after he died and telling me that they had left things for me. I liked their furniture just fine. I had always slept on their couch when I visited and thought it very comfortable. It felt like they wanted me to have it. "I'd like the furniture, if that's okay," I told my dad.

He was having their things packed up by a company and made the arrangements to ship a bunch of their things to me. I would pay for the delivery upon arrival with the money I had inherited from them. The only problem was, the furniture would arrive in a little over a month, and I lived in a tiny, albeit almost empty, apartment. Where was I going to put everything? My grandparents had lived in a one-bedroom apartment as well, but theirs had been much larger than mine. I decided that I would just pile things up along the walls until I could find a better solution.

Some weeks later I saw a maintenance person in the

apartment across the hall. I said, "Hi," and then noticed that the apartment was empty. "What happened?" I asked.

"They were evicted. They hadn't paid their rent."

"Who's moving in there?"

"I don't think they've it rented yet. The people just moved out yesterday; the place is a mess."

"Did they take the snake with them?"

"Yup. No snake–it's gone. Don't worry."

I thought that they must have moved out while I was at work. I decided to go over to the leasing office and see how much more expensive that apartment would be. It cost over two hundred dollars more than what I was currently paying. "I can't afford that," I told the leasing agent. I don't know whether she just liked me or whether they had too many vacancies, and it would be easier to rent my apartment than the two-bedroom one, but she gave it to me for one hundred dollars more than what I was currently paying.

She told me that they would need to make a few repairs, paint, and clean the place up before it would be ready for me. When she told me the day that I would have to take it over I was really surprised–it was the day before my furniture was scheduled to arrive. I've never had an easier move. I walked my few things across the hall into the freshly painted apartment and welcomed my grandparent's furniture the next day. The delivery people placed everything exactly where I wanted it. I slept well in my new room on the quiet side of the building and set up an office in the spare room so that I could get my work done more effectively.

I still have my grandparents' furniture, and it's in daily use; I think of them just as often. Thank you, Grandma and Grandpa, for your gifts and for helping everything work out so perfectly. Thank you for all of it, actually. Thank you for helping to take care of me when I was little, for the Early Bird dinner specials, for the trips to Florida to visit you–for everything.

Red Sky at Night,

Sailor's Delight

I had been promised a second husband–the keeper, and my angels were true to their word. How I met Owen, the long series of events that led to our finding one another, needs more time and space than I can give it here. I guess I'll just have to write another volume of "Tales" to tell that miraculous story, among many others.

I remarried five years after Pete died. This time I knew that I'd met my match–on so many levels. Owen works even harder than I do, which is a fairly impressive feat. When I tell him that I love to work, he doesn't look perplexed. Instead, he gets it. He found his calling earlier than I found mine, and has dedicated himself to it for decades, thoroughly enjoying himself. As those who teach, who were meant to teach, know, teaching is as much of a calling as a summons to ministry.

Suffice it to safe that our meeting was against all odds and impossible and clearly guided. When Owen told me, "We're so lucky that we found each other," I had to laugh.

"We definitely did not find each other. Left to our own devices, we never would have met."

"Yeah. I guess. I just mean that we're lucky."

"We're lucky, but I don't think that luck had anything to do with it. God brought us together. I think that he just couldn't watch anymore."

"What do you mean, 'He couldn't watch anymore?'"

"I don't think he could stand it. The thought of watching us try to date without his guidance was probably more than he could bear. I know I'd had it."

Owen, a hardened skeptic when we married, has become so intuitive that increasingly he takes the lead, letting me know what he's receiving when I'm feeling stuck or disconnected. We now make a great, non-reluctant team.

The Lifeboat

Owen and I had been married for a few years, teaching at the same school, and generally using our vacations to visit family, especially our parents, as they began to enter older age. It was Spring Break, and I had gone to visit my parents and Owen had headed to visit his. I was driving with my mother, about to enter the Beltway, a human construction I've never been able to navigate–how in the world am I supposed to tell if I'm driving on the inner or the outer loop? It all loops!

Suddenly, a loud voice interrupted our conversation (of course, only I heard it as my mother continued to chat away) that told me that Owen was about to be in a terrible car accident.

"Mom, Owen's about to be in a car accident! I have to call him!"

Mom, whose hearing was failing pretty badly by this point, hadn't heard me at all and continued to tell me her news.

"Mom, I have to call Owen, he's about to be in an accident!"

Mom continued to talk, and I quickly realized that I didn't have time to explain to her that I needed to cut her off in order to call Owen. Ignoring her (to this day I couldn't begin to tell you what she was telling me–all of my attention was diverted, fully, to trying to alert my husband), I called Owen who I knew was driving on a highway on which the legal speed limit is often 75 miles per hour.

"Owen! Slow down! You're about to be in a terrible car accident!"

"What? Hi. What are you talking about?"

"No! Slow down now! You're about to be in a car accident!"

"What?"

"Slow down! Slow Down! Watch out! You're about to be in an accident!"

We hung up, and I started to pray furiously. Mom was watching me, wondering what was going on. A few minutes later I got a call back from Owen.

"You meant me! You meant that I was about to be in an accident!"

Since the sound of his voice told me that he was completely okay, I decided to express disbelief and frustration rather than concern. That felt really close. That was scary!

"What part of, 'YOU are about to be in a terrible car accident' didn't you understand? When I said 'YOU,' who did you think I meant?"

"It's just that it didn't make any sense. You couldn't see me. The traffic was all flowing just fine, everything seemed great, but I did what you said. I started slowing way down, and then everyone around me must have thought that I knew something that they didn't, so they all slowed down next to and behind me as well. The traffic I was in slowed down, and when we came around that big curve before my exit off the Interstate, we were able to stop in time. Many of the cars that had made that turn a little before us had been able to avoid joining the collision ahead of them, but now that traffic was stopped almost to the curve so there wouldn't have been time to do anything, and we would have gotten crushed in a second pile-up."

"Owen's okay," I told my mom. "He's okay. He listened to the warning and he's fine."

As I write these words years later, I give prayers of thanks yet again, perhaps for the thousandth time, to those unseen beings, those angels and guides and ascended masters and saints and whoever they might be who saved Owen's life and prevented so much tragedy that day. "Thank you, God."

Although I had predicted many, many things for Owen, and for myself, and for our lives in general, in those first years of our marriage, and although he was learning to listen to and beginning to trust the voices I heard and the guidance I received, that event marked a true turning point, both in terms of our relationship and in terms of his intellectual, scientific stance. He became more flexible, opening his mind and paying attention to the world beyond his personal thoughts. He began to listen.

Owen knew that there was no way I could have understood the developing driving conditions in a state 2,000 miles away, deciphering a situation he and the other drivers around him knew nothing about. Something else, something beyond, something greater than us individuals with our private concerns and personal and limited view had interceded, protected, and guided us that day.

The Life Saver

Driving is tricky, and one is so dependent on the wisdom and good behavior of the other drivers circling and swirling around you, sometimes like a school of fish moving in unison, sometimes like a shark seeking prey. Some of my most emphatic and clearest forms of guidance have occurred while driving.

One summer Owen and I were making our way from visiting family in New England to my parents further south. We were just past New York when I started getting a strong message that there was going to be a big accident, and that if we wanted to avoid it, I needed to be the one to drive and I needed to pay close attention to all signals given to me. That evening was some years before my cross-continental call to Owen telling him to slow down, and as I explained to Owen that I was seeing a big car accident coming, he seemed skeptical. I told him that I was hearing that I needed to be the one to drive because the message to pull off, to slow down, to swerve into another lane, or whatever the guidance might be, would probably come suddenly and would need to be followed immediately. I wouldn't have time to receive and then try to explain to him what evasive measures I was getting that we needed to execute instantly. He was unconvinced, perhaps, but agreed that it was my turn to drive.

We headed onto I-95, and the warnings were getting louder, although not specific. I was incredibly focused as I drove carefully down the middle lane, ready to do whatever I was told. I prayed for us and for our car, I prayed to be able to hear and understand any guidance given, I prayed for help in following whatever I would be shown, and I prayed for all of the other cars and trucks, drivers and passengers on the roads that night.

"Dear God, please keep us safe. Please help us drive really well and with respect, care, and consideration. Please help us be alert, focused, defensive drivers. Please protect us." On and on the prayers went in my mind.

After that evening of fear and red alert, and on similar occasions, I've asked questions along the lines of, "Why not just guide us to spend the night in a hotel rather than risk danger?" "Why not instruct us to take a route through the Pennsylvania hinterlands instead?" "How about telling us to leave earlier or later rather than having us pursue our course in the midst of danger?"

Just like the night when the man climbed in my fourth story window to attack me, there have been other times when I've had a scary or difficult or even a really nasty experience and I wasn't warned about it, or I wasn't warned about it sufficiently to avert it, only to be prepared to face it. In those instances I've gotten angry at these guiding and protective beings, wondering why I couldn't be spared hardship, terror, and pain. I wondered why, if I could hear them so clearly, wasn't I being spared an unhappy experience? Yes, often I was led to avoid the entire situation, but sometimes I was guided to the sidelines of an event and at other times I was seated right in the middle of the fray.

The answers I have received over the years have been patient and consistent, and this experience was no different. It has been made clear to me that I agreed to this lifetime and accepted as part of it that I would be presented with certain challenges, lessons, and hardships from which I could learn important lessons if I chose to face and embrace the pain and the fullness of the experience. Avoiding the difficult experiences would set me back on my path since it would be through the challenges that I would learn and grow the most as a human being.

Secondly, I was told, firmly, that I was learning how to listen and learning how to follow. Again, I had agreed to this path in advance, and at times it was going to be arduous. The path required that I learn, eventually, to follow, to absolutely follow, in every single area of my life and without question, the loving, albeit at times forceful, directions I was given.

I was told that I would only ever be given guidance that was positive, loving, kind, wise, and helpful. Never, ever would I be told to do something in which I would be led to hurt myself or another person. The loving kindness and gentleness that I experienced around any guidance received would assure me that I was following a God-given path and not one prompted by any form of darkness.

The Lighthouse

Driving in the fading light along I-95, I was still learning to follow.

Doing my best to be alert for all signs in the midst of heavy traffic, I suddenly had a sharp, stabbing pain in the bunion on my right foot. I'd felt a bit of discomfort there before, but it had never really pained me in the past. Now it felt like a knife was jabbing me in the side of my foot. The pain was so intense that I didn't even recognize it as the sign I'd been looking for. Instead, I was absorbed in hurting and in wanting my foot to stop hurting. "My bunion is killing me," I told Owen. "I'm going to pull off at the rest stop ahead."

From that day forward that bunion periodically hurt like hell, and the one on the other foot soon followed suit, causing pain to the extent that within a couple of years I decided to have surgery to remove them. On that night, though, my bunion served as a messenger.

The awful pain "coincidentally" preceded one of the rare exits for a rest stop on I-95. This exit was from the left-hand lane because the stop was located between north and southbound traffic. I left I-95, parked, and we decided to take a little stretch break. After bathroom, coffee for Owen and a tea for me, and taking a walk inside the building to let the pain subside in my foot, we headed back toward the exit. We stepped outside and were confronted with what we hadn't seen or heard from inside the bustle of the rest stop.

All traffic was at a complete stop in both directions. The sounds of different kinds of sirens filled the air as rescue vehicles approached, their target to our south. Ambulances, fire trucks, and police rushed to help those they could in the mangled wreckage we would soon witness, an 18-wheeler having landed on a car now almost obscured from sight amidst destroyed vehicles and lives cut short. We stopped in our tracks and just looked at each other for a moment.

"Thank you, God," I said, over and over again. It's become the refrain to accompany my life, and it's one that I don't think I can say often enough. "Thank you, God."

The next step, of course, was to pray for the healing, blessing, guidance, protection, and comfort of all those involved.

Scrubbing the Deck

While driving or preparing to take a trip, there have been numerous other times when I've been guided to slow down, to leave the house a bit earlier or later, to take a different road to my destination, or to postpone an errand for another day. Sometimes I've arrived at an accident after it had already occurred, other times, as it was being cleared up, or perhaps I heard or read about it later on and realized that I had been led to avoid the situation completely.

Some years ago my husband and I were driving along the Oregon coast, taking a vacation to celebrate our 10th wedding anniversary. By this time Owen had had enough experiences with me to trust that any guidance I received should be heeded carefully. When I started to have a vision of a car accident that was going to occur in front of us, his immediate response was, "You drive."

We pulled over to switch drivers and we prayed together for our safety, our car's safety, and for the safety and well-being of all those who were driving along Oregon roads. At times we prayed and at other times we enjoyed the beautiful scenery and talked about whatever came to mind. The images I was receiving were persistent, although they were becoming somewhat less drastic, so we maintained our vigilance, prayed periodically, and remained alert to any guidance we might receive.

After another couple of hours of driving, we saw an appealing state park with access to the ocean. We paid and parked and hiked over the dunes to the wild beach beyond. It was a beautiful day, and we stopped to enjoy the views, to wander around and walk the coast for a bit, and to take some pictures. When we got back in the car, the images returned, but they were different. The accident had happened.

Just a few miles down the road the traffic was stopped, emergency vehicles were on the scene, and cars were being diverted onto an alternate route away from the bridge over which the road we were on traveled. As we drove on the side road we could see that a serious accident involving at least a couple of cars had occurred. The bridge was quite narrow, and there would have been very little room in which to manoeuver. We gave thanks for our safety and guidance and prayed again for those involved.

Both shaken and relieved, we arrived at a little town just past the bridge and pulled into a gift shop that sold items made from wood, including from myrtlewood. We explained to the lady behind the counter that we had just been diverted around the road because there had been a car accident on the bridge. The poor woman had a horrified look on her face, and her coworker immediately ran over to comfort her. They began to call family and friends in the area to make sure people were okay and to try to learn what had happened. It turns out that the woman we first spoke with had lost a family member to an accident some years earlier in approximately the same place. My silent prayers turned to comforting her.

The next day we logged onto the local paper to read about the accident. Although a man who apparently had lot of drugs in his system at the time had lost control of his vehicle on the bridge, and in the process had hit the side of the bridge and a couple of cars, his was the only fatality. After glimpsing the accident on the bridge, and remembering the far worse images I had initially envisioned, that outcome felt miraculous. Yes, that man had caused his own death, but he hadn't caused death or major harm to anyone else. The original scene that had been presented to my mind had transformed, perhaps in part through our prayers, to a much less drastic outcome and to one that didn't involve us at all. My belief in the importance of listening, of following, of praying, and in expressing gratitude continued to strengthen, and it has continued to deepen ever since.

These many "non-accidents," or accidents in which I wasn't directly involved, have led me to pray every time I get into a car, not just for myself, for my car, and for any passengers I'm carrying, but for the cars, roads, and travelers wherever I happen to be, and beyond. Often I include prayers for airports, planes, ports and boats, trains, and other forms of transport. Almost every day I pray for my home town, its citizens, and the surrounding counties and states, as well as for this country and for the world. In short, I pray a lot and for a lot of different things. I'm a very different person than I was as a teenager and in my early 20s, clinging, although rapidly losing my grip, to a secular and scientific worldview.

Fog Horn

I never did manage to have children. Owen and I tried, but I could never escape the first trimester before miscarrying. During those years of so much hope and loss, I was heart-broken each time I'd start to bleed, each time a doctor told me that there was no longer a heartbeat to be heard.

I'd cry deeply and then throw myself back into my teaching and the rest of my life.

The voice I'd heard in college that tried to get me to kill myself, the one belonging to a former student who had once lived in my dorm room, was correct. That deceased student had caused a lot of pain and hardship, both to me and to previous inhabitants of that room. Unfortunately, though, he was right about my not having children.

I would have liked to have kids myself, but one of the biggest lessons I've had to learn has been: "What is, is."

Sometimes, it's just that simple, stark, and straightforward.

Perhaps, if I'd followed the early directive I'd received to move to Santa Fe, I might have given birth to children myself as well as have step-kids. Maybe, if I'd listened to my guides better they would have taken me on a course that would have led to some different outcomes in my life, such as trying to have children when I was younger.

But, what is, is. I can't know what would have been or could have been.

Instead, like everyone else, I've been encouraged to make peace with those parts of myself and those aspects of my life that aren't as I wished they were.

Before I met Owen, I heard a voice say, "You will have children at 38." A couple of weeks after my second marriage I remembered what I'd heard and realized that, at age 38, I now had three step-children. True, they were young adults, but they were still my children. The voice had spoken truly.

At the same time, I'd hoped to have the experience of giving birth to and raising a child myself. Instead, I was asked to be wiser than that.

Biology, I've come to realize, often has little to do with whom we come to regard as members of our family. Whether through marriage or adoption or other sorts of communities and comings-together, many of our lives are richer and more complex and less ordinary than simple nuclear family units.

I am reminded of the fact that there already are enough children in the world. Instead of raising a small child, I have time to write my books and to complete the work that the angels have placed before me. Maybe I'll even finally fulfill the call to ministry I received so many years ago.

As I've come to understand, they're all our children.

Starry Night

In early September of last year I dreamt that my mother died. In this vivid dream we hugged each other and were happy as we reminisced before she crossed over to the other side. We knew it had been a good life as we reviewed her time here together, her life a story of overcoming and adventure and accomplishment. She was ready to go and at peace, and despite some tears, I woke up smiling and feeling contented.

I looked over at the clock by the bed to see the time. It was way too early to get up, but as the dream faded a bit I began to worry, its elation leaving along with it. Had my mother really died that night? It felt like we had been saying our good-byes. Our interaction and conversation in that dream-space had felt so real to me. I checked in quietly, asking if she'd really passed away. It felt like she probably hadn't, but I wasn't sure. I felt happy about the dream, but also a bit worried. "It's okay," I decided, "Just go back to sleep."

I woke up again a short time later having had almost the exact same dream. Again, I felt elated about the time Mom and I had spent in that dreamscape, but now, awake, I was more concerned. Had she departed that night?

"That's significant," I thought. "An instant replay. That almost never happens."

My husband was sound asleep beside me, which was

reasonable since it was about 2am. I got up and went downstairs, alternating between feeling upbeat, sad, and worried. My mom had seemed so happy during the dream, and we'd had a wonderful time getting ready for her to go.

When my husband got up–and fortunately he's a really early riser–I told him about my dreams. He was similarly concerned. We waited until it was a reasonable time to call and discovered that she was fine.

By fine, I mean, "alive" and ticking. Mom hadn't been "fine" for some time.

The Calm Before the Storm

I can't prove that my mom and I had a real encounter in another dimension, but our conversation and contact had looked and felt genuine. Her conscious mind might have wanted to live a lot longer, but I suspect that her Higher Self didn't and that it was preparing her, and me, for the next step in her journey. I think of the Higher Self as the aspect of our being that helps to prepare our lifetimes before they begin, guides us, as permitted from beyond, during the course of our lives, and with which we are reunited when we "die." There is no such thing as death, right? Many of us have learned this by now. Sometimes we oscillate at lower frequencies and become visible to the naked eye; and at other times we oscillate much more quickly and are invisible, at least to those who aren't able to perceive the more refined and subtle frequencies of the heavenly realms.

Mom had had a really bad fall the year before my dream, fracturing her leg high up near where it meets the hip. It was a tricky and painful fracture that required significant recovery time. Somehow in the fall she also lost the hearing in one ear. Given the fact that the hearing in the other ear wasn't very good, she was now more cut off from people than before because it was much harder for her to follow a conversation and to communicate effectively with others.

She'd been through cancer, and although she'd recovered a few years earlier, her health had never been robust since the radiation treatments. She had pulmonary hypertension. She had congestive heart failure. Additional health issues competed for her time, attention, and resources. For the last couple of years one of her doctors, a lovely man with whom she liked to joke, had been telling her, "I don't know why you're still alive. With everything that's going on with you, I really have no explanation!" They would laugh about that, about how she could possibly still be ticking along, however precariously.

I'd been praying for her extensively and doing a lot of energy work on her for many years, but intensively over more recent years. My theory of how she was still alive at least three years past reasonable expectation involved God's healing presence in our lives, the energy work I did on her almost every day, and the answering of prayers.

She wanted to stay alive, for more than any other reason, to be able to meet her granddaughter, her first grandchild. That goal had been accomplished, but now she hoped to see her turn one, maybe even two.

I'd been traveling more often to see her and help out, but I lived far away. She'd never wanted to move in with us or even to move close by, no matter how hard I tried to convince her otherwise. The first time she visited the town she said, "It's dead here! Where is everybody?" It was about nine in the evening, and she had a point. She was a city girl. She had her own life and friends. She wasn't about to move to snow and wilderness and mountains. So I commuted, as best I could, when we had breaks in the school year and as finances permitted.

About three weeks after my dream, Mom fell again. Luckily she was able to drag herself to the phone to call for help in the middle of the night. At the hospital they completely missed the triple fracture in her pelvis. She was in terrible pain, and the hospital was trying to release her. My brother got her admitted to a rehab facility, but with her diagnosis of no fracture, they didn't take her pain seriously either and were trying to get this elderly woman to walk around and to do physical therapy, no less!

We told the doctors that she could complain about anything and everything else, but she'd lived through war. Pain was just not something she complained about. Even when she was given pain pills, after a knee replacement or after dental surgery, she might take one or two pills the first day, and that was it. She'd rather just tough it out. The poor lady suffered until my brother, a persuasive guy, got them to medicate her properly. Then her potassium dropped like a stone and she almost died before being readmitted to the hospital where, under pressure, the staff did the appropriate scans this time (once she was out of the ICU and strong enough to handle more tests, that is) and found the triple fracture–three weeks late.

She went through so much during those last months. It's distressing to see patients kicked out of rehab facilities before they're ready, to watch them not being listened to or taken seriously, and to see the large gaps in our care for and caring of the elderly.

Mom returned to rehab. She returned to the hospital, to another rehab facility, and then the hospital again. As the months wore on, the chances of an actual recovery were looking slimmer and slimmer, but at least she had some time to get to know her granddaughter a bit. Their bond was intense, the toddler never afraid of the lady with tubes trailing from her body.

Land Ho

During those last months of her life in which Mom was in rehab, got C-diff, and went through so many trials, cheating death a couple of times before the end, she began to speak of dreams she was having in which she saw her parents, her brother, and other people who had already crossed over.

My father-in-law, too, in the months before he passed away, at times would speak of seeing his mother and other people.

I'm not suggesting that my mother or father-in-law were somehow unique in this regard–quite the opposite. Instead, it is now commonplace and even expected, among those who care for the very ill and dying, to witness their patients begin to speak with beings they cannot see, to have unusual experiences, conversations, and visions which make perfect sense to them even if the people caring for them don't understand what is being described, and to talk of dreams they had in which they were visited by people no longer on earth.

The veil between worlds or realms becomes thin, I believe, at the beginnings and endings of our lifetimes. That's why babies often seem to shine with a light and peace beyond this world. That's why the room in which someone has just died often feels especially still; a reverence lingers in that space. As the filmy divide between this world and the next becomes increasingly transparent, information is more easily received and voices are more effortlessly heard and understood.

I also believe that those near death often travel back and forth between different dimensions, returning to describe those they encountered during their visits on the "other side." People in a coma, likewise, are probably traveling much of the time between our dimension or reality and other realms.

Cutting the Life Line

Mom had fallen out of her chair at the rehab facility and was taken to a hospital nearby on Friday. Nothing was broken, and she wasn't in pain. I was planning to come out to see her in a week when my Spring Break started, but the next day I got a call from my brother saying he'd just heard from the hospital that she was going down fast and that he and his wife were making the five-hour drive from where they were that night. Meanwhile, he called a close friend of his to sit with her, just in case he didn't get there in time. This friend had been through enough loss in his life to feel comfortable sitting with someone at the very end. It helped that he was also someone she thought of as one of her own.

For a number of months we had hired a woman to sit with her and help her out on weekdays as well as a person to help on weekends. Right now the lovely weekend person was with her, and she offered to stay late with Mom, but we wanted "family" to be with her as well.

Meanwhile, my husband and I were on the computer and phones trying to get me a flight during a key Spring Break week–not my break, but it was clearly "head to the mountains to ski week" for a lot of people. We couldn't find a flight, even though we were even looking at possible departure cities several hours away from where we lived. I was starting to panic when someone must have cancelled his plans. I got a flight out of our town for the following afternoon. I'd get in late Sunday–early on Monday

301

morning, actually, but it was the best I could do.

My brother and sister-in-law had spent Saturday night with Mom. My brother stayed in town while his wife left to pick up their daughter from her parents. I arrived around 1am on Monday, slept a bit, and then that morning my brother and I went to the hospital. I'd been praying that Mom would hang on long enough for me to see her again. I was really anxious on Saturday, but by Sunday morning I felt her promise that she would wait for me, and I relaxed a bit. Now we were on our way to the hospital; it didn't allow visitors into the ICU on Monday mornings. We got there at 11, just as we were allowed in to visit.

Mom knew us and managed to say my brother's name even though talking was almost impossible for her at this point with all of the equipment hooked up to her. We stayed with her into the afternoon when she suddenly started to fail in a more drastic and permanent way.

We held her and told her we loved her as we sent her into the Light.

"Mom, we love you. Thank you for being our mother. Thank you for everything. You've had a great life. It's time for you to go now. Head straight into the Light. Go to the Light."

It was hard to tell the exact moment when she left her body because she had a pacemaker that kept the monitor beeping while the oxygen machine kept pushing air into her lungs.

"I think she's gone," I said.

The nurse, who'd stayed with us throughout these last minutes, had tears in her eyes as she checked for vital signs. The holy moment of death had touched us all.

We were facing Mom's form lying on the bed when suddenly we heard a whirring sound, "Rrrrr. Rrrrr," coming from behind us.

I turned around to see the light flashing on the paper towel dispenser a ways behind us by the room's exit. The paper stopped and then the "Rrrrr, Rrrrr" happened again as the light flashed and some more paper rolled out of the machine. There was no one anywhere near the dispenser. Let me amend that. There was no one visible to us standing anywhere near the dispenser.

We knew that that was her message to us, a kind of waving good-bye so that we'd know that she was heading out of the room to destinations beyond our reach.

I loved her good-bye signal to us. It was clear that she was the only one who could have made paper come out of the dispenser, twice.

I can't think of how many times I've performed little dances in bathrooms around the country trying to get a paper towel to show itself. I'll wave my hands in front of it. I'll swipe my hands back and forth in front of the stubborn machines. In my experience, it's not easy to get paper out of those things, which are motion-sensitive, but only to the right kind of movement in just the right location.

Gabrielle, the bride whose bouquet toss years before had been accompanied by a voice telling me that my first husband would be taken from me, had developed cancer to which she'd eventually succumbed. She regretted leaving three children behind, but finally had to move on despite still being young enough for one of her children to be a toddler.

Gabrielle's mom told me that the family had gathered around Gabrielle's bedside, holding her as she passed away. A few moments later, the wind chimes downstairs on the front porch began to ring, her parting "wave" good-bye and "see you soon" to her family still standing around her body in her second floor bedroom on that utterly still and windless evening.

I've heard of butterflies landing on caskets, of music suddenly beginning to play from a device that wasn't even turned on, of rainbows, of dream visitations, of smelling the scent of the perfume worn by the one who has passed, and of whisperings, visions, and even the touch on the shoulder or a kiss on the head as the deceased person leaves the body behind and heads into the Light.

Our loved ones need to go, as we all do, when the time comes, but they work hard to let us know that they're okay, that we don't need to worry about them, that our grieving should, at some point, come to completion.

Dolphins Swimming

in Our Wake

A friend of a friend, let's call her Joyce, came to see me. Joyce and I had met before but barely knew one another, and it had been some time since we'd seen each other. She wanted to talk and to see what I received about her mom. She didn't tell me that her mother had recently passed away, not wanting to stack the deck, I suppose, but I told her that it felt like her mother had passed, which she confirmed.

Weirdly, it can be difficult to tell whether or not someone has died. Sometimes, when a person died a few years before, they have taken on new bodies and so they feel really alive even though their previous existence came to a close.

The issue is, death doesn't exist. Many people who've crossed into the Light, say after a bad accident, and then were sent back by their angels because they still had work to do in that particular lifetime, not only report, consistently, that they didn't want to return to their bodies, they also often say that while they were "dead" they'd never felt so alive.

Consciousness continues uninterrupted. It doesn't matter if we're asleep–our minds still think and our spirits are still learning and interacting with ideas, with people, and with information. It doesn't matter if we seem to be in a coma–we are still thinking and can hear what is going on around us. People who have awakened from comas have reported being aware of what was happening to them and of what those visiting and caring for them were saying.

It isn't different when we leave our bodies. We are still thinking our thoughts and still have feelings and opinions. We still feel the life within us, the life that we are. It's not our bodies that make us alive. We are not our bodies–they simply house us for a time. We are energy beings made of light, and our existence departs the body to return to the realm from which it entered that body prior to birth.

I asked Joyce if her mother had died from cancer, which she confirmed. I received a few messages for her from her mother, but the main thing that her mother kept saying was, "You know. You know that you know."

I repeated this to Joyce, who would simply nod her head, and then we'd speak of something else until those words echoed in my mind again, and I'd have to tell her, "Your mom just keeps telling me to tell you that 'You know. You know that you know.'"

I felt a bit silly saying, "You know" over and over again, but her mother was insistent that those words would be meaningful and clear to her daughter even if they seemed vague and unimportant to me.

Finally, it felt like the transmission from her mother was complete, and I thanked her mother as I said good-bye.

"Did that make sense to you?" I asked Joyce. "Was that meaningful to you?"

"My mom and I had been really close, and it was so

hard for me to lose her. I asked her to give me a sign from the other side so that I'd know that she'd made it and was doing okay."

"We didn't have a specific sign that we'd agreed upon. She just kept telling me that I'd know it when I received it. 'You'll know,' she'd tell me. 'You'll know.'"

"Mom and I had that conversation a couple of times with her reassuring me that I would know the sign when it came."

"Then you kept saying she was telling you, 'You know. You know that you know.' That was her message to me before she left, and it was her message to me again today."

I thought that that was such a simple and beautiful way to confirm her continued existence and well-being to her daughter while reminding Joyce that faith was key, that her own intuition would guide her (in this case to seek me out), and that their connection could not be severed by something as ephemeral and nonexistent as death.

In the end I've decided that no matter what happens, no matter what we experience during our lifetimes, we are all meant to be whole. It cannot be God's will for us to be fragmented and tormented beings eking out a lifetime, simply surviving through our existence despite our traumas and partings and regrets and pain. We are meant to be whole. We are meant to receive all of the gifts, from grief and loss to joy and rejoicing. We are meant to rebuild our spirits after sorrow and to seek and affirm the good and the holy throughout our lives.

The Sextant

It can be so difficult to let go of those we love and so hard to trust that they're okay, that they continue on, even if we've seen or felt ghosts around, even if we've received messages from the other side, even if we have a deep faith in an afterlife. I think that my dream with my mother was so joyful because she was moving on to a much brighter, more brilliant, and happier place.

Yet I'm often not sensible. I've cried tears of grief over my mother, my father-in-law, my first husband, and countless other friends and family members. I've cried at the death tolls from earthquakes and tsunamis in which thousands, none of whom I'd ever met, had perished, and I've cried over the loss of a pet.

That's the human side. Even if we know perfectly well with every fiber of our being that the person we have "lost" is feeling happier and more contented than we are perhaps even capable of, we still can't see them, touch them, or sit down to dinner or talk over the day with them as we might have in the past. We experience a loss while they experience a gain. They have the opportunity to return to the Light from which they came, and when they do so I believe that they do not experience a longing to return to our world or to the lifetimes they've just left.

"What if they committed suicide?" I'm often asked.

I have talked with many people who have worried

about loved ones who had killed themselves. I believe that we are meant to face our lives as they appear and to consistently work to surmount struggle and to overcome problems during those periods in our lives when hardship shows up; every life contains at least some truly painful moments and harsh challenges. I also believe that the difficult times will teach us the most, helping us grow and deepen. The soft, easy, gentle times comfort and soothe us, and the unhappy ones catapult us forward on our paths.

I believe that suicide is the wrong choice, and every person who has committed suicide with whom I've spoken on the other side has always profoundly regretted their actions. At the same time, everyone is God's child, and everyone is welcomed home with loving and open arms, prodigal sons, all of us, by a cherishing and forgiving Father.

I've seen many "mansions" on the other side with varying characteristics and degrees of brightness. I truly believe that everyone is admitted into the Light, but the experience of "Light" might not be as bright for one person as for another. That's okay. We're not done just because we've completed a human lifetime. We're eternal beings. We have so much more to learn and experience.

In the case of suicide, the person who died, once reaching the Light, has the opportunity to continue to heal, to grow in kindness and compassion, and to experience more and more of the Light, of Wisdom, of Goodness, and of Truth. All mistakes are forgiven and all foolishness overlooked as we are made whole in the holiness, the wholeness, of the Light.

It was a surprise to me the first time I deliberately spoke with someone on the other side for a friend whose mother had crossed over. I discovered that she was really busy. I've encountered people in Heaven who work with babies and children who have died. I've seen others helping soldiers, often from both sides of a given conflict, soothing them after what was probably a sudden and violent death, helping the soldiers acclimate to their new surroundings, helping them to let go of and make peace with the past, and assisting them as they moved forward.

When teaching, at times I would feel the classroom fill up with other attendees in addition to the physical forms clearly visible before me. I must be talking about something important, I would reflect, if all of these departed souls were brought here, instantaneously, to listen to what I had to say. Just because one is no longer on earth doesn't mean that the lessons don't continue.

I've seen souls gather around while I was having a deep conversation with family or friends. I've seen giant lecture halls on the other side where people gather to study and grow. Some people choose to be guides to their earth-bound loved ones during their human lifetimes, others assist in whispering wisdom, comfort, and help to people on this side, whether they ever knew them in the past or not. The jobs selected are those that best suit a person's abilities, interests, areas for growth, and the continuing development of wisdom and insight.

I don't believe that we're ever done learning and growing. Nor do I believe that the earth is the only place into which one can incarnate to proceed on one's journey. I just don't much believe in many limits at all anymore.

The Flagship

What did my mother say to me after she had crossed? She told me she loved me, she apologized for the hard things she'd said and done, for her mistakes, and she talked about the different people she had seen and whose company she was able to enjoy once again. She visited my classrooms, interested to observe how I taught and what I was teaching. After a little while, though, her message was for me to let her go.

"Move on. Keep moving forward. Live your life. Let me go. You need to let me go so that I can move on fully and so that you're free to live your life fully as well. I love you. We'll talk from time to time. Pursue your goals and plans. You're doing great!"

Mom has been actively present during the writing of this book, prompting me to write and write. She's enjoyed watching this book unfold in its telling and has learned more about my experiences and perspective of being psychic, from my days of resistance and reluctance to my current stance of actively embracing the guidance received.

I've asked for her forgiveness for every thoughtless and unkind thing I've ever done or said to her–and there were plenty. I've worked to forgive her for her misdeeds as I've sent her blessings, gratitude, and light as she continues to ascend on her path. I've worked to let her go as I strive to release the anxiety, egoic point of view, personal sense of limitation, and other forms of smallness in myself.

What can we learn from death? How to live.

Life is imbued with a sense of purpose as we learn to live with gratitude and with a connection to forces larger than ourselves. We open to wisdom and to our inner depths and life become meaningful and magical.

As we let go of our fear of death, we develop our ability to live whole-heartedly and to live in a manner that is fully engaged with others and with the world. We actively seek out opportunities to be of service. We want to develop our potential and use the gifts we were given to accompany us during this lifetime. We want to honor the good, the gentle, the witty, and the wise wherever and whenever we encounter it. If we're really listening, we realize that the sacred resides within us and surrounds us in every holy instant.

Shipshape

Those times when I opted to follow the guidance I received, I would find myself having more than the ordinary number of useful and fun coincidences because I would somehow unconsciously know the perfect time to leave the house in order to run into a friend. I'd happen across a going-out-of-business sale in a part of a city I'd never been to before and find that the store was clearing its shelves of exactly what I needed. I'd avoid a traffic accident. I'd find myself in the right place in the right time and, equally importantly, I wouldn't be in the wrong place at the wrong time.

I would know which job to apply for or what to say to comfort a friend. I didn't make a lot of money, but I discovered an ever-growing sense of contentment and inner peace. I seemed to be on a path that, when I consented to follow it, was focused on figuring out how I could be helpful to others and how I could learn and grow as a human being.

If the voice outside myself is the lunch counter lady with a hairnet as well as wings, what is the inner voice's source? Of course, I have no definitive answer here any more than I do about what is behind the loud, commanding voice, but I have come to think of the inner voice as my "Higher Self" or soul. I see the Higher Self as that part of me which existed before my birth and will continue on after my death. The Higher Self is aware of its existence in God and remains connected to eternal truths. On the other hand, my small self is constrained by my limited personality constructed of problems, self-consciousness, and ego. The small self has a name and personal identity. The Higher Self is beyond names and labels of any kind. The little self has needs and wants, opinions and moods. The inner voice, the Higher Self, is connected to and remembers the Light.

My path has been, and continues to be, one of releasing and overcoming the small sense of self to embrace my Higher Self in my daily life. As I have become more and more psychic, I have been able to express more and more of my psyche as I move through the world, remembering the sacred in the midst of the mundane.

The word *psychic* has the same root as the term *psychology*. In Greek the "psyche" is the soul, so the field of psychology refers to the "study of the soul." At last, I've embraced my psychic abilities. My psychic gifts help me to lead a wiser, safer, more meaningful life; they guide me to be of service to others, and they serve the soul. Rather than studying my ego or personality or small, separated self with its endless list of complaints, demands, and problems, I'd rather dedicate my life to connecting to my soul, to learning from it, to becoming more soul-full.

This Higher Self has been helpful in the daily running of my life, guiding me as I navigate the ordinary, as I steer through the shallows of my mind. Lunch counter lady intervenes for the big stuff, and Higher Self takes care of everything else. At least, that's how I understand it today. I'm indebted in ways beyond counting to both of these forces that have taught me, comforted me, protected me, and instructed me in my developing sense of compassion and insight.

There's nothing special about me. We are all

continuously receiving guidance from beings with greater vision and wisdom than our own. But are we paying attention? Are we willing to listen?

Will we follow?

Ship's Captain

In the end I can only conclude that we are not the captains of our own ships. We never were, no matter what we told ourselves, and furthermore, we were never meant to be in charge. True power lies beyond us.

As we grow in wisdom, we let go of our false beliefs, gradually releasing the illusions and childish imaginings that held us back and that constituted an immaturity of thought and a resultant immaturity of action.

Instead, as we evolve we seek out maps to help us chart our course and navigate the depths in our lives. We consciously and willingly relinquish the helm. We no longer kid ourselves that we are meant to be the masters of our own lives. Most of our lives and being occur beyond our understanding and conscious thought. Something greater than ourselves built our bodies, maintains them, and gives life to us and to all around us. The intricate beauty of galaxies beyond counting and universes parallel and infinite, the ability to reflect on the expansive and the complex, to fall in love, to dedicate our lives both to others and to grand ideas, our capacity to demonstrate devotion, to express kindness and to feel compassion–these abilities all speak to the great mysteries, point toward holiness, signal the divine.

Something far greater than ourselves would like to help us steer a truer and happier course. I finally understood, in the core of my being and without the will to resist it for another instant, that it would be a very good idea to dissolve my little will into infinite purpose and design.

We aren't in control, so we can stop pretending that we are. Being controlling is unpleasant anyway. No one likes it when other people are controlling–it's neither a successful personal nor interpersonal strategy.

What's exciting is that as we let go of all of our attempts to control ourselves and our lives, others, and the world around us, something else finally has the room to step in and much more actively chart our course. We let go, and the miracles begin to manifest. We release certainty, and the beauty of uncertainty fills us instead. We gradually loosen our hold on our treasure trove of facts and beliefs as genuine wisdom and deeper understanding replace them.

Miracles have more space to appear in our lives; peace and a sense of well-being increase because we are no longer trying to live from the perspective of our false selves, as a persona through the lens of a problematic personality.

Instead of talking all of the time, we begin to listen. Instead of thinking we know, we ask questions and become more comfortable with mystery and uncertainty.

Our intuitive gifts, waiting in the wings for our readiness, begin to manifest in our lives as we develop the understanding and maturity to handle them. These psychic abilities are then able to give us the signs and teachings that guide us to live more happily and successfully, to protect us and keep us safe, and to be more helpful and cooperative in the world. We recall the truth of our origins in the divine, dedicate ourselves to respecting the value of our lives, and glimpse the beauty of our final destination.

Clear Sailing

The language of the divine reaches us through the refined channels of intuition, its communication being so much more enlightened and expansive than mere words and the limitations imposed by our personal thoughts.

How can we develop our intuitive gifts? Here are some suggestions:

- Stop trying to control things.

- Value happiness over certainty.

- Let go of the need to be right.

- Ask lots of questions.

- Pray for help and guidance.

- Express gratitude.

- Meditate.

- Sit in silence and simply listen.

- Pray for healing, wisdom, and truth.

- Let go of the past.

- Return your mind to the present again and

again and again.

- Give the future to God.

- Practice forgiveness.

- Release judgment of others.

- Be kind to yourself.

- Choose to be helpful when you can.

- Express a generosity of spirit.

- Let go of fear.

- Release limiting beliefs and negative words and behaviors.

- Decide to be compassionate, tolerant, open-minded, and respectful.

- Give thanks to God for your life, because it is a gift beyond our ability to comprehend.

- Choose peace.

Watch the miraculous manifest in your life.

About the Author

Mari Schoenzeit lives with a view of trees, the trans-dimensional cat, Cecil, by her metaphysical side. She has taught school and worked as a massage therapist, now turning her attention to fulfilling an early directive received as a child to become a writer. She still hasn't responded to her call to ministry and has not yet learned how to sail, but hopes that, as with the guidance to write, the missive received to enter the ministry doesn't have an expiration date. For now she is a landlubber, working on becoming increasingly grounded, centered, and present. Time spent navigating inner landscapes has given her glimpses of stars.

It is Mari's goal to encourage others to listen to the wisdom within and to follow the healing guidance and direction received from beyond the personal. She hopes to inspire others to connect more deeply to their authentic selves as they chart a meaningful course through their lives.

Recommended Readings

A Course in Miracles, published by the Foundation for Inner Peace.

Made in the USA
San Bernardino, CA
22 May 2016